CATALOGUING

A GUIDEBOOK

Sparse on examples
NUC dismissed in a couple of ⨍o.

LC rules 2p,   p.7 c
79. LC no longer summarize title
     editor statement?

Compare with Dunkin' Cataloging USA

p.81 new, simplified code in prep.?

84 lib. school diffs.
         Rules not to be memorized.

Pr. test   94 rule 142-Br
in dicer   95 due for pub in 74
cat.

95-96 repeat AACR to be pub in 1974
94 examples = Br not am.
100 Br. opinion as to multimedia
104 LC films —

                    From
113 Microforms   does not
     compare Canadian with
     departs from AACR

122 queer heading
125 SBN - unique no - new idea?
127 Derek Austin ?
129 SBN arr. MARC records

130 3d ed MARC info
141 obviously?
        ar

1 + notbook
mention of
summaries.

2 best known
LAFR2 ?
3 mention of
role of LC.
new rules.

MARC not
panned as
stand. of format

CATALOGUING

A GUIDEBOOK

*Being a revision and rearrangement
of Patrick Quigg's 'Theory of cataloguing'*

by

ERIC J HUNTER

MA FLA AMIET

Lecturer, Liverpool Polytechnic

LINNET BOOKS & CLIVE BINGLEY

Library of Congress Cataloging in Publication Data

Hunter, Eric J.
    Cataloguing: a guidebook.

    " A revision and rearrangement of Patrick Quigg's
' Theory of cataloguing.' "
    Bibliography: p.
    1. Cataloging. I. Quigg, Patrick Joseph. Theory
of cataloguing. II. Title.
Z693.H85 1975   025.3   74-13599
ISBN 0–208–01362–8

FIRST PUBLISHED IN THE UK 1974 BY CLIVE BINGLEY LTD
THIS EDITION PUBLISHED IN THE USA 1975 BY
LINNET BOOKS, AN IMPRINT OF SHOE STRING PRESS INC,
995 SHERMAN AVENUE, HAMDEN, CONNECTICUT 06514,
PRINTED IN GREAT BRITAIN

CONTENTS

5

1*

ACKNOWLEDGMENTS

My thanks are due to colleagues on the staff of the Department of Library and Information Studies at Liverpool Polytechnic for helpful comment and advice.

ERIC J HUNTER

INTRODUCTION

The period since the publication of the second edition of Quigg's *Theory* over five years ago has witnessed a great number of changes in the cataloguing world.

The Library Association syllabus, to which *Quigg* was directly related, has been extensively revised and, indeed, has assumed a much reduced rôle. Library schools in the UK now have their own varied syllabi and carry out their own internal examinations and assessments. For these reasons, the opportunity has been taken to rearrange *Quigg* to form what is considered to be a more logical pattern. The view is taken, for instance, that the student should be aware not only of the *purpose* of the catalogue but also of its *appearance,* both with regard to outer physical form and the inner arrangement of entries, *before* progressing to study the history of, and influences upon, catalogues of various types.

With regard to techniques and methods, the influence of the computer has become far more marked. This has led to some quite radical changes, one example being the introduction of the 'microfilm cassette' catalogue. There are also other innovations such as the remarkable ultra-microfiche bibliography *Books in English* and automated indexing systems such as PRECIS. ' Computerisation' can no longer be relegated to a 'final' chapter, but must be introduced at a much earlier and vital stage so that it can take its rightful place as an integral part of the current library process.

Rapid progress in the media industry has posed problems for the librarian in that he must now concern himself with a variety of new forms of library materials, each presenting certain special difficulties with regard to identification, description and indexing. The basic objectives of cataloguing, which for so long have remained unchanged, must perhaps be restated to take account of these factors.

The present text has therefore been extensively revised to include contemporary development.

A further interesting feature of recent years has been the publication of several comprehensive treatises on cataloguing, including Horner's *Cataloguing* (1970), a new edition of Needham's *Organis-*

ing knowledge in libraries (1971) and Bakewell's *Manual of cataloguing* (1972). It is not the intention of this work to replace these but rather to complement them by serving as an introductory guide to the subject. It will of course, in addition, update much of the information that they contain.

Southport, 1974   ERIC J HUNTER

BASIC READING LIST

To obviate the necessity for constant repetition of the bibliographical details relating to books which are cited upon more
than one occasion, such details are given here and the work is then
referred to in the text by the abbreviation shown in the left hand
column.

Some of these works are obviously 'dated' and will not provide
an accurate picture of the current cataloguing scene. Essential
readings from this point of view are asterisked.

Bakewell   *Bakewell, K G B: *A manual of cataloguing
practice* (Oxford, Pergamon 1972).

Coates   Coates, E J: *Subject catalogues: headings and
structure* (London, Library Association 1960).

Foskett   *Foskett, A C: *The subject approach to information* (London, Bingley: Hamden, Conn, Linnet
2nd ed 1971.)

Horner   *Horner, John: *Cataloguing* (London, Association of Assistant Librarians 1970).

Jolley   Jolley, L: *Principles of cataloguing* (London,
Crosby Lockwood 1960).

Needham   *Needham, C D: *Organising knowledge in libraries: an introduction to information retrieval*
(London, Deutsch 1971).

Norris   Norris, Dorothy May: *A history of cataloguing
and cataloguing methods, 1100-1850; with an
introductory survey of ancient times* (London,
Grafton 1939).

Olding   Olding, R K: *Readings in library cataloguing*
London, Crosby Lockwood: Hamden, Conn,
Archon 1966).

Pettee   Pettee, Julia: *Subject headings: the history and
theory of the alphabetical approach to books*
(New York, H W Wilson 1946).

Piggott   Piggott, Mary *ed*: *Cataloguing principles and
practice: an inquiry* (London, Library Association 1954).

Rowland	Rowland, Arthur Ray: *The catalogue and cataloguing.* A collection of essays. (London, Crosby Lockwood: Hamden, Conn, Archon 1969.)
Sharp	Sharp, Henry A: *Cataloguing: a textbook for use in libraries* (London, Grafton 4th ed 1948).
Shera and Egan	Shera, Jesse H and Egan, Margaret E: *The classified catalog: basic principles and practices* (Chicago, American Library Association 1956).

When a reference is cited in the text merely by the author's surname followed by (*op cit*), eg *Mason* (*op cit*), this indicates that full bibliographical details are given in the reading list provided at the end of the particular chapter.

Textbooks cannot possibly keep pace with new developments and professional journals therefore become essential reading. Among those that are particularly relevant in cataloguing are:

Catalogue and index
   The periodical of the Library Association Cataloguing and Indexing Group. Quarterly.
International cataloguing
   The bulletin of the IFLA Committee on Cataloguing. Quarterly.
Journal of library automation
   The official publication of the Information Science and Automation Division of the American Library Association. Quarterly.
Library resources and technical services
   The publication of the Resources and Technical Services Division of the American Library Association. Quarterly.
Library of Congress   *Information bulletin*   Weekly.
Library of Congress   *Processing Department   Cataloging service bulletin*   Irregular.
Program   An ASLIB publication which provides news of computers in libraries. Quarterly.

VINE: a Very Informal NEwsletter on library automation
   Produced by the OSTI information office for library automation. Three or four issues a year.

A useful irregular series of articles on 'Cataloguing and indexing activities' appears in the *Library Association record*.

ABBREVIATIONS USED OR REFERRED TO THROUGHOUT THE TEXT

AA	Anglo-American
AACR	Anglo-American Cataloguing Rules
AAL	Association of Assistant Librarians
ADP	Automatic Data Processing
AECT	Association for Educational Communications and Technology
AKWIC	Author and Key Word In Context
ALA	American Library Association
BIBLIOS	Book Inventory Building Library Information Oriented System
BL	British Library
BLCMP	Birmingham Libraries Co-operative Mechanisation Project
BM	British Museum (now part of the British Library)
BNB	British National Bibliography (to be part of the British Library)
BNFC	British National Film Catalogue
BRIMARC	BNB/Brighton Public Libraries catalogue project
BUFC	British Universities Film Council
CAIN	Cataloging and INdexing system
CAML	Canadian Association of Music Libraries
CARDS	Card Automated Reproduction and Distribution System
CAS	Chemical Abstracts Service
CIP	Cataloguing in Publication
CIS	Cataloguing in Source (now CIP)
CLA	Canadian Library Association
COM	Computer Output Microfilm
COMP	Computer Output Microfilm Peek-a-boo
DC	Dewey Decimal Classification
DILS	Dataskil Integrated Library System
EMAC	Educational Media Association of Canada
EVR	Electronic Video Recording

GDR	German Democratic Republic
HELPIS	Higher Education Learning Programmes Information Service
HMSO	Her Majesty's Stationery Office
IBM	International Business Machines Corporation
ICCP	International Conference on Cataloguing Principles
ICL	International Computers Ltd
IFLA	International Federation of Library Associations
INSPEC	Information Service in Physics, Electrotechnology and Control
INSPEL	*International newsletter of special libraries*
INTREX	INformation TRansfer EXperiment
ISBD (M)	International Standard Bibliographic Description (Monographs)
ISBD (S)	International Standard Bibliographic Description (Serials)
ISBN	International Standard Book Number
ISDS	International Serials Data System
ISSN	International Standard Serial Number
KWAC	Key Word And Context
KWIC	Key Word In Context
KWOC	Key Word Out-of Context
LA	Library Association
LASER	London and South Eastern Region interlending service
LC	Library of Congress
MARC	MAchine Readable Catalogue
MEDLARS	MEDical Literature Analysis and Retrieval System
MINICS	MINimal Input Cataloguing System
MIT	Massachusetts Institute of Technology
MUMS	Multiple Use Marc System
NCET	National Council for Educational Technology (now Council for Educational Technology of the UK)
NCL	National Central Library (now part of the British Library)
NLL	National Lending Library for Science and Technology (now part of the British Library)
NPAC	National Program for Acquisitions and Cataloging
NRCd	National Reprographic Centre for Documentation
OSTI	Office of Scientific and Technical Information (now part of the British Library)

PCMI	Photo Chromic Micro Image
PICA	Project Integrated Cataloguing Automation
PRECIS	PREserved Context Indexing System
RECON	REtrospective CONversion of catalog records
SBN	Standard Book Number (more accurately ISBN)
SLIC	Selective Listing in Combination
SWULSCP	South West University Libraries Systems Co-operation Project (now SWALCAP South West Academic Libraries Co-operative Automation Project)
UBC	Universal Bibliographic Control
UDC	Universal Decimal Classification
UK	United Kingdom
UKAEA	United Kingdom Atomic Energy Authority
UN	United Nations
UNESCO	United Nations Educational, Scientific and Cultural Organisation
US	United States of America
VDU	Visual Display Unit
WADEX	Word and Author inDEX

CHAPTER ONE

GENERAL HISTORY (1)

The history of cataloguing can be considered from several viewpoints, notable contributions made by librarians, the influence wielded by institutions, societies and conferences, the development of catalogues of various kinds and the development of codes of rules and practice. These various aspects will be referred to where appropriate throughout the text of this work. Such references will generally be confined to events of the ninteenth century, when it might be said that modern cataloguing practice really had its beginnings, and the twentieth century.

Prior to this, the catalogue most usually performed the function of a mere inventory of stock, which contrasts sharply with its present rôle as a systematically arranged tool facilitating the use that can be made of a collection of library materials.

The history of the earlier periods is dealt with by *Norris*. She includes an 'introductory survey of ancient times' and recognises that, chronologically, catalogues fall naturally into four groups:

1 Ancient catalogues to AD 1100, ' Scanty material, difficult to find, frequently contradictory ';

2 Medieval monastic catalogues 1100-1400, of which she says ' it would be impossible to describe more than a few ';

3 Collegiate (or academic) catalogues 1400-1700 (three chapters, including one on the Bodleian Library catalogues);

4 Catalogues from 1700 onwards, including a chapter on the British Museum catalogues.

Norris ends her study at this point in time, when the influence of certain outstanding librarians, such as Panizzi of the British Museum, was about to make itself felt and the way in which the art of cataloguing was to continue to develop into the twentieth century was about to be shaped.

READINGS
Bakewell p 14-16.
Sharp Ch 25 'History of catalogues'.

Strout, Ruth French: 'The development of the catalog and cataloging codes' *Library quarterly* 26 (4) October 1956 254-275 (*also in Rowland* p 3-32). This essay begins with an explanation of the origin of the word 'catalog' and surveys the history of cataloguing from 'one of the oldest lists of books of which we have knowledge', a Sumerian tablet found at Nippur and dated about 2,000 BC, to the beginning of the twentieth century.

CHAPTER TWO

PURPOSES OF CATALOGUING

Catalogues have for long been generally accepted as indispensable tools, but recently the basic, challenging question 'Do libraries *need* catalogues?' has been mooted. (See, for instance, M W Grose and M B Line 'On the construction and care of white elephants: some fundamental questions concerning the catalogue' *Library Association record* 70 (1) January 1968 2-5; Richard Bennett 'Catalogues and classification—are they necessary?' CIIG *bulletin (Construction Industry Information Group)* 1 (5) October 1971 9-15; and D J Urquhart 'On catalogues' *NLL review* 1 (3) July 1971 80-84).

Bakewell, an able and persuasive advocate of the catalogue, nevertheless agrees (p 13) with the suggestion made by Grose and Line that 'we need to make a serious study of the uses and functions of the catalogue', and he hopes that 'the survey of catalogue use organised in 1971 by the Cataloguing and Indexing Group of the (British) Library Association will provide helpful information'. The results obtained from this survey (Arthur Maltby *UK catalogue use survey.* London, Library Association 1973) in fact indicate that only 30 per cent of public library members actually use the catalogue. Corresponding figures for university and college libraries are 77 per cent and 62 per cent respectively. Bryant and Needham, in reviewing Maltby's work (*Catalogue and index* (30) Summer 1973 16), point out that a significant factor is whether guidance has been received on *how to use* the catalogue. Where such guidance has been received, 84 per cent of the recipients (in all types of library) make use of the catalogue, whereas only 52 per cent of those who have had no guidance use it. For public libraries only, the corresponding figures are 78 per cent and 36 per cent respectively. These are interesting ratios which indicate that when readers *are* made aware of the way in which a catalogue can help them, then the great majority *will* make use of it. Grose and Line would, of course, state, as Bakewell notes, that: 'we have so arranged our libraries that it is almost impossible to find books, whether specific, or on a given subject, without' a catalogue!

Despite the provocative attitude adopted by Grose and Line, the fact remains that books, documents and other material in a library collection can each be physically arranged by *one* factor only. For books, the most consistent and useful arrangement is by subject, or perhaps, as in the case of fiction, author. A variety of other approaches may, however, be used in seeking material in a collection. On the catalogue, therefore, falls the burden of providing, by means of multiple entries, the necessary access.

The full library catalogue should be an instrument equipped to deal with the several principal channels of enquiry and it is of essential importance to the successful identification and retrieval of books, documents etc, no matter what pattern of arrangement is applied to material on the shelves.

One hundred years ago, Cutter defined the purposes of the catalogue in his *Rules* thus:

1 To enable a person to find a book of which either: *a*) the author is known, *b*) the title is known, *c*) the subject is known.

2 To show what the library has: *d*) by a given author, *e*) on a given subject, *f*) in a given kind of literature.

3 To assist in the choice of a book: *g*) as to its edition (bibliographically), *h*) as to its character (literary or topical).

Cutter's objectives *a*) and *c*) are indisputable. Objective *b*), while usually interpreted, in the case of works with personal authors, to cover only significant or striking titles, also includes all those documents for which the title entry would be the principal one, *eg* periodicals.

Objective *d*) encounters the difficulty of such traditional problems as authors writing under different pseudonyms, successive changes of name, etc. These problems have generated many rules in many codes.

Objective *e*) might nowadays be amplified to cover not only the ' given subject ', but also ' related subjects ', although Cutter's (and the dictionary catalogue's) focus on specificity is perhaps reflected here.

Objective *f*) covered by ' form entries ' is usually approached on a selective basis, since the amount of material that can be entered under a form heading such as DICTIONARIES can be vast.

Objective *g*) is covered by the descriptive cataloguing of the work and there is much evidence of heart searching by cataloguers throughout the years about the desired fullness of description in relation to the purposes of cataloguing.

Objective *h*), a matter of notes and annotation, can nowadays rarely be achieved in a large catalogue except perhaps, as in the case of *f*), on a selective basis.

Nevertheless, Cutter's examination of the aims and purposes of cataloguing remains substantially valid, and later statements are usually re-statements of them.

Mary Piggott, reporting the findings of the 1961 International Conference on Cataloguing Principles, says 'Cutter's objectives, in so far as they relate to author entry, remain unchanged' (*Assistant librarian* 55 (11) 1962 212).

It should be noted, however, that library's now concern themselves with a variety of media in addition to the book form and when Cutter's objectives are considered, they should be viewed in this light. They could, perhaps, be restated thus:

1 To enable a person to find an item of which either: *a*) the person or body having primary intellectual responsibility is known, *b*) the title is known, *c*) the subject is known.

2 To show what a library has: *d*) by a given person or body, *e*) on a given subject, *f*) in a given kind of literature or form of material.

3 To assist in the choice of an item as to *g*) its physical form, *h*) its content and character, *i*) its edition.

A briefer statement of the objectives of the catalogue, which still seem relevant, is provided by *Shera and Egan* (p 9): 'The conclusion from both experience and analysis seems inescapable that there are two basic functions of the catalog that are of outstanding importance: 1 accurate and speedy determination of whether or not an item known by author or title is in the collection, and, if so, of where it may be found; and 2 what materials the library contains upon a given subject and where they may be found.'

Where books are concerned, this statement suggests a lessening of the bibliographical identification function (Cutter's objective *g*), which is increasingly being shouldered by 'published bibliographical services'.

Most of the discussion on catalogue function will nevertheless be found to be centred on debating, evaluating and perhaps modifying one or more of the objectives stated by Cutter.

Some of the questions that have to be asked concern:

1 The possible ' inventory' function of the catalogue which, while probably the original function, is now almost obsolete in the light of the shelf-list.

2 The conflict between the catalogue as an uncomplicated ' finding list ' for the location of specific books, and the catalogue as a bibliographical instrument assembling ' groups ' of books under uniform headings. Paul Dunkin's remarks are worth reading on this point, in his explanatory commentary which runs as parallel text in S Lubetzky *Code of cataloging rules: an unfinished draft* (ALA 1960 p 9 to 15).

3 Following upon this, the possible relation of the catalogue function to that of the general bibliographical apparatus.

4 The conflict that may exist between the catalogue functioning as a working tool for the professional staff and as an instrument available to the general reader.

Question 2, finding list versus bibliographical instrument or reference tool, provides, perhaps, the most vexing area of enquiry in the light of constantly increasing cataloguing costs. There is some evidence that the ' finding list function ' has gained a slight advantage in the debate. The University of Oxford *Report of the Committee on University Libraries* (Oxford, 1966), otherwise known as the *Shackleton report*, which examines the situation regarding libraries and catalogues in Oxford impressively, and at length, states in measured terms (Par 320), '. . . the question should be asked, is a library catalogue to be regarded as a series of irreproachable bibliographical documents, or as a means of finding books? We take, without hesitation, the second view.' In International Conference on Cataloguing Principles, *Paris, 1961 Statement of principles,* annotated ed, with commentary and examples by Eva Verona assisted by F G Kaltwasser, P R Lewis, R Pierrot (London, IFLA Committee on Cataloguing 1971), it is noted (p 8) that 'some delegates expressed the opinion that the functions' of collocating works by a particular author and identifying editors 'might be omitted, as not being important for all alphabetical catalogues'. The new *Anglo-American cataloguing rules, 1967* with their emphasis on what might be called the ' user-oriented ' heading, the form of name by which the author, personal or corporate, is *commonly* identified, might be claimed to this extent to be shaped towards acceptance of the fact that the catalogue should function firstly as a finding list.

Again, the continuing and accelerating movement towards the automation of library processes, has brought a fresh approach to bear on the question of catalogue function. The required careful analysis of those operations involved in computerisation tends to produce a situation in which such analysis cannot be confined merely to the operations themselves, but must extend to their purposes and to their ends. In the automated library, the catalogue lies at the very heart of the system, and consequently its form, function and purpose is being subjected continually to constant re-examination in innumerable library automation conferences, institutes, workshops, and working parties. Ritvars Bregzis ' The Bibliographic Information Network: some suggestions for a different view of the library catalogue' chapter nine, p 128-142 in *The Brasenose conference on the automation of libraries* argues that the computer can produce a ' reactive catalogue ', that it can generate from a common bibliographical data store, a *system* of catalogues that are all mutually compatible and fully mechanised with transference from one to the other being easily effected. One generated catalogue might serve the finding list function (' the bibliographic data form orientation '), another might be generated, whenever required, to serve the requirements of ' bibliographic data correlation ' *ie* providing a catalogue serving as a bibliographical tool assembling literary units. A somewhat similar view is put forward by R W Macdonald and J McRee Elrod in 'An approach to developing computer catalogues' *College and research libraries* 34 (3) May 1973 202-8 (see also p 37).

Such a development, which has been made even more feasible by the flexibility already achieved by MARC (see p 129) and other computerised systems, would finally resolve the conflict of purpose and function in this area of the library catalogue.

It should perhaps be stressed from the beginning that the same cataloguing principles are applied not only to the entry of items in library catalogues but equally to the entry of items in bibliographies and other works involving 'listing' and 'identification' such as indexes and abstracts. The essential difference between a catalogue and a bibliography does not lie in the format and

arrangement of entries but in the fact that the former *catalog* is restricted
in that it relates to one particular library or group of libraries,
whereas the latter takes no heed of library locations but may be *bibl*
restricted in some other way, for example it could be confined to
items dealing with a particular subject, or published in a particular country, etc.

READINGS

Bakewell Ch 1 'The nature and purpose of cataloguing'.

Coates Ch 3 'The two-fold objective'.

Horner Ch 2 'The need for catalogues'.

Jolley Ch 1 'The function of the catalogue'.

Olding Lubetzky's statement of objectives and implications p
249 and the editor's prefatory note to this reading p 243-4.

Shera and Egan Ch 1 'The nature and function of the catalogue'.

CHAPTER THREE

PHYSICAL FORMS OF CATALOGUES

The manner in which the library catalogue can be made available for use by the reader has produced a number of ' physical forms ' of presentation.

The printed book catalogue

In this the entries are printed as text in a conventional book-form catalogue available in multiple copies.

Features: It is the easiest form of catalogue to use, and the most acceptable and comprehensible to the greatest number of people. It can be guided with great clarity by manipulation of typography and layout. A printed page of entries can be scanned with greater speed and less error than any other arrangement, and its ' portability ' and multiplicity of copies offer great advantages.

Problems: It is highly expensive when produced by conventional printing methods and, in a growing collection, is out of date immediately. It offers no possibility of insertion or interpolation of entries for new material, which can be indicated only by way of supplements, and this then produces the problem of ' several places to look '. The problem of ' withdrawals ' can only be met by producing new editions at regular intervals.

The printed book catalogue as a viable form appeared to die the death in the early years of this century when, in libraries large and small, it was replaced by the new more flexible card catalogue (although there were a few examples of printed catalogues available, notably those of Liverpool and Glasgow). Yet, technological advance appears to be turning the wheel full circle. Newer methods of printing allied with photography and offset lithography have shown that the entries on cards or slips in the catalogues of large research libraries or collections (with little or no withdrawal problems) can be efficiently transformed into book-form catalogues, as has been done on a fairly extensive scale by the G K Hall Company for the catalogues of many specialised libraries and collections and, on an even larger scale, by Mansell for the catalogues of the British Museum and the *National union catalog: pre-1956 imprints*. The availability of such catalogues in book form has added a new dimension to the bibliographical apparatus of libraries acquiring copies. It also led to many large libraries considering the possibility of reducing the bulk of their card catalogues at a certain date to book form, and perhaps supplementing this with entries in a card catalogue.

F A Sharr 'Book-type catalogues for developing countries' UNESCO *Bulletin* 20 (1) Jan-Feb 1966 24-26 and 'The production of a new book-type catalogue in Australia' *Library resources and technical services* 10 (2) Spring 1966 13-14 has described how the book form catalogue for the Western Australia State Libraries was produced without using particularly expensive equipment, by means of short entries typed on Kalamazoo Copystrip and reproduced from litho plates. Again, the computerised cataloguing system, with its ability to store entries, to interpolate new entries, erase withdrawals and produce printed-out up-dated versions of the catalogue in book form at suitable intervals, has led to a revival of the oldest form of catalogue by means of the newest method of preparing catalogues.

The automated production of printed book catalogues

Kelly L Cartwright notes the three major categories of book catalogue production systems in which machines may be utilised, and provides examples of American libraries which use, or have used, these methods in his paper 'Automated production of book catalogs' (In Preconference Institute on Library Automation, *San Francisco, 1967 Library automation: a state of the art review;* edited by Stephen R Salmon. Washington ALA 1969) viz:

1 EAM systems, *ie* electronic accounting machines. This method uses punched cards, which can be sorted mechanically, and the information thereon is then printed out by use of accounting machines ready for reproduction by photography or offset printing. This system has been used by Los Angeles County, Baltimore County, King County (Washington), University of Rochester and the New York State Library.

2 Sequential camera systems. Entries are typed on cards upon which further information is punched, thus allowing these cards to be sorted and collated by machine. A camera photographs the

typed portions of the cards in sequence. The product is a photographic negative which is cut and formatted into pages and printed out by a photolithographic process. This system has been used by Fairfax County (Virginia) Public Library and the Los Angeles County Library.

3 Computer systems. Basically, these can be considered as having a three part operational sequence:

(i) The production of machine readable input on punched cards, punched tape, or magnetic tape.

(ii) The manipulation of the data base, *ie* the information which has been input. This is done accurately and with great speed.

(iii) The output, which can be utilised in several ways. For instance, the computer print out itself can be used as a 'master' and then reproduced by xerography on some other method. Photocomposition may also be used, the page master in this case being a photographic negative.

Florida Atlantic University, Stanford University and Harvard University are examples quoted by Cartwright of libraries using computers for catalogue production.

The machines used in the first method are limited in scope and anything that can be done on them can be done far more efficiently by computer. Certain libraries have, therefore, been known to abandon this method in favour of (2) or (3).

On the other side of the Atlantic, it was mainly the large research and academic libraries which tended to lead the way where computerisation was concerned. Computers were first applied to library techniques in the early 1950's, Taube's post-coordinate indexing system (see p 152) proving eminently suitable for mechanisation, but the first application of computers to cataloguing processes was not to come until some ten years after this. The first proposal for a single machine readable record from which multiple products, such as printed catalogue cards and subject bibliographies, could be obtained was probably that of L R Bunnow in a report for the Douglas Aircraft Company: *Study of and proposal for a mechanised information retrieval system for the missiles and space systems engineering library* (California, Douglas Aircraft Co 1960). The automated production of catalogue cards began in 1961.

E Heilinger 'Applications of advanced data processing techniques to university library procedures' [Illinois] *Special libraries* 53 (8) October 1962 472-475; J M Perrault 'The computerized book catalog at Florida Atlantic University' *College and research libraries* 25 (3) May 1964 185-197; R De-Gennaro 'A computer produced shelf list' [Harvard] *College and research libraries* 26 (4) July 1965 311-315, R Bregzis 'The Ontario new universities library project—an automated bibliographic data control system' *College and research libraries* 26 (6) November 1965 495-508, are all representative of early patterns of development. Subsequently there have been, as *Bakewell* (p 154) states, 'innumerable articles on the production of book catalogues by automated methods in the United States professional press, notably *Library resources and technical services*'. Recently, however, this flood seems to have dried up somewhat.

The history of library computerisation in the United States from its initiation in 1954 to 1970 is described by Frederick G Kilgour: 'History of library computerization' *Journal of library automation* 3 (3) September 1970 218-219. This journal is in fact a very useful source of information on current computer based cataloguing activity in the us. Typical of recent articles are 'BIBLIOS revisited', by John C Kountz 5 (2) June 1972 and 'Multipurpose cataloging and indexing system (CAIN) at the National Agricultural Library', by Vern J Van Dyke and Nancy L Ayer 5 (1) March 1972 21-29. The first of these articles updates earlier reports on the Orange County Public Library's BIBLIOS (Book Inventory Building Library Information Oriented System). This is an integrated system covering acquisitions, processing, cataloguing and book fund accounting. The first edition of the BIBLIOS book catalog was released in May 1971 and cumulative supplements were issued six times in the first year. Output options include production of either cumulative supplements or a full catalogue. The second article deals with an interactive system which, with a single keyboarding of data, provides all necessary catalogue cards, book catalogues and related internal reports as well as a computer data base for information retrieval.

The first computerised catalogues in Great Britain were produced by public libraries, the London boroughs leading the way when they were faced with the problems of amalgamation in the 1960's. W R Maidment describes the Camden attempts at computerisation in 'The computer catalogue in Camden' *Library world* 67 (782) August 1965 40. This brief article sums up thus: 'The computer catalogue seems to be the only conceivable way of securing the advantages of a union catalogue in book form for a large system of libraries'. Another early computerised catalogue was that of Barnet; A C Meakin describes the system adopted and discusses the advantages and disadvantages in 'Production of a printed union catalogue by computer' *Library Association record* 65 (9) September 1965 311-316. Both the Camden and the Barnet catalogues were produced by International Computers Ltd on a service basis. These pioneer catalogues were somewhat 'primitive' productions in that they were usually confined to restricted entries in capital letters with little punctuation. Nor were they devoid of 'teething' troubles; the Camden cumulations, for example, actually ceased to appear for a while in the early seventies due to programming difficulties. Gradually, however, problems are being overcome and it is now possible to produce catalogues by computer giving a more sophisticated layout with fuller entries in upper and lower case letters.

Other British public libraries which have become involved with automation of library catalogues include West Sussex (from 1964), Greenwich (from 1965), Flintshire (from 1968), Coventry (from 1969), Cornwall (from 1970), Bournemouth (from 1971) and Lancashire (to become operational in 1974).

West Sussex County Library claims to be the first public library system in the UK to have used data processing for book charging. This was introduced at Chichester in 1967. Much earlier than this, in 1964, work began on the creation of a limited catalogue data base. The 'mini-catalogue' produced was, due to programming limitations, not the ambitious union catalogue, with full entries, envisaged but it served as the only form of public catalogue until 1970. Then began development of an automated system for the complete integration of stock records, catalogues and issue methods. This system is now established and is described by R J Huse in 'The West Sussex Libraries catalogue and information system' *Library Association record* 75 (7) July 1973 127-130. The basis of the system is the creation of a Master Catalogue File and use is made of MARC tapes. The adult non-fiction catalogue is printed annually and these annual volumes are kept up to date by supplementary cumulations (an author sequence is issued every two weeks and a classified sequence every four weeks).

The computer used by Flintshire County Library is an expensive IBM 360/30 machine, but it is claimed that sharing the computer with the County Treasurer's Department has kept financial consideration of computer cataloguing to an advantageous minimal level (Glyn Davies 'Computer cataloguing in Flintshire' *Library Association record* 72 (5) May 1970 202-203). In Flintshire, it was decided at the outset to computerise the catalogue records in sections, beginning with adult non-fiction. Whilst computer processing of new non-fiction additions to stock is carried out regularly, processing of records of older stock is also done simultaneously according to machine availability. Monthly cumulative supplements of new title additions are produced; and copies of the computer printed catalogue are distributed to all branch and mobile libraries in the county.

Bournemouth Public Library's system was designed around the inexpensive Olivetti RP 50.* The primary concern here was book charging but it was decided that 'to use a computer solely for this simple function seemed to be neglecting an opportunity to integrate it with cataloguing and possibly other housekeeping aspects of library administration' (Bournemouth Library *A computerized library system* Bournemouth, 1971 p 2). This is a sensible and now widely held viewpoint and it must be stressed that it is now the exception rather than the rule for libraries to concern themselves with the computerisation of a single process. There are three library processes which are readily adaptable to automation —'ordering', 'cataloguing' and 'circulation'. The present tendency is for these to be 'integrated', with the catalogue as the focal point to the system.

In simple terms, the basic requirements of any such system are:

1 A computer file recording information relating to items in stock or on order.

2 A computer file recording information relating to the registered readers.

3 A unique number to identify each item and a further unique number to identify each reader. These numbers are used when

---

* The RP 50 is apparently no longer in production. Olivetti are of course developing other equipment. One machine which should prove extremely useful to cataloguers is the DE 523. This is a direct data entry machine which incorporates a keyboard and a VDU and which produces a mini cassette of magnetic tape.

communicating with the computer. They can be used, for example, to check whether a particular book is in stock or on order.

4 The necessary programs to search, manipulate, print out, etc, the files.

Where ordering is concerned, the computer can be programmed to print orders, to send reminders and perform other routine tasks, cataloguing can be done in various ways as described in this chapter.

For circulation systems, issue records consist of a machine readable file of numbers relating to items borrowed and the corresponding numbers of the readers who have borrowed them. Such records can be made by having special tickets for both book and reader, each ticket containing a machine readable number. These numbers can be recorded at the issue counter by special machines or, in the case of the Plessey system, by a 'light pen' which 'reads' numbers optically represented by what appears to be a series of lines of differing widths. Programs are available for overdue notices to be automatically printed by the computer and reservations can also be handled automatically. Where the latter is concerned a visual, *ie* a light, or some other indication will be triggered off whenever a required book is 'checked-in'.

Statistical and other 'management' information can also be readily obtained from such systems.

To return to the Bournemouth system, a monthly cumulative print out of the author section of the catalogue is issued and complete copies every six months. Bournemouth Library does not claim that this system is the best in library computerisation but it is believed that it is relatively cheap and also economic in operation.

Many British academic libraries, in Bath, Birmingham, Essex, Liverpool, Loughborough, Newcastle, Southampton, etc, are now experimenting with computerisation. Some like Bournemouth Public Library, regard computer produced catalogues as a secondary aim. This is so, for instance, at Essex University, where the library's main current interest is the design and implementation of an on-line* circulation system.

* On-line systems are linked directly to the computer which can thus be utilised immediately and at any time for processing. A visual display unit, which is similar to a television screen, is usually employed. Off-line means that the computer can only be used at certain times. This limits utility and flexibility and material must be processed in 'batches'.

Interesting work is being carried out at Bath University, where the library started production of a machine readable 'mini-catalogue' in 1971, minimal input with maximal flexibility of output being the aim (Philip Bryant and Maurice Line 'Cataloguing and classification at Bath University Library . . . *Library Association record* 73 (12) December 1971 225-227). A report on progress at Bath was issued in 1972: *The Bath mini-catalogue: a progress report,* by Philip Bryant, Gillian M Venner and Maurice B Line (Bath University Library February 1972). Bath was one of the universities participating in the South-West University Libraries Systems Co-operation Project (SWULSCP),* the main aim of which was to investigate the feasibility of sharing computers as an economic and efficient means for automating library systems and services. (See R F B Hudson and M G Ford *South-West University Libraries Systems Co-operation Project: a report for the period July 1969 December 1972* University of Bristol 1973).

Loughborough University of Technology has been developing an automated systems approach, including MINICS (Minimal-Input cataloguing system) since 1966 and significant advances have been made. A status report by R A Wall appears in *Program* 6 (2) April 1972 127-143, and R A Wall, M E Robinson and D E Lewis report further in MINICS (*Minimal-Input Cataloguing System*) *development report* (Loughborough University of Technology 1973).

For those librarians considering conversion of their catalogues into computerised format, a useful reading is A E Jeffreys *The conversion of the catalogue into machine readable form* (Newcastle, Oriel Press 1972). This work is the final report of an OSTI project carried out at the University of Newcastle.

Computerisation of cataloguing processes is not confined to the United States and Great Britain. In Canada, for example, a 'tri-regional' computer produced book catalogue was developed in Ontario to help ease the 'serious' cataloguing problems. The system is described by P P Hallsworth in 'Tri-regional computer produced book catalogue' *Ontario library review* 57 (1) March 1973 18-20. A further article by Margaret Galloway appears in the same issue 21-23.

Another example can be found in Holland where PICA (Project Integrated Cataloguing Automation) aims to establish a common

* Now known as SWALCAP (South West Academic Libraries Co-operative Automation Project) and Bath University no longer participate. See also p 39.

data base for all Dutch university libraries. Borrowers will be able to 'converse' with the data base. See 'Automatisering i Holland; en introduktion af edb-projekterne PICA og RANDTRIEVER' *Bogens Verden* 54 (8) 1972 565-569.

Where the use of computers for cataloguing (and other library housekeeping activities) is concerned, the librarian has the choice of:

1 Operating completely independently.
2 Working in co-operation with other libraries.
3 Using a national service.
4 Any combination of these.

In Britain, OSTI has encouraged studies of the various alternatives and reports of progress are given in the OSTI *Newsletter*. C M Overton reviews the projects in 'The OSTI supported library automation projects' (*Program* 7 (4) October 1973 181-195). The use of a national service would relate to MARC (MAchine Readable Catalogue), which involves subscribing libraries being supplied with cataloguing entries on magnetic tape, and this service is discussed in chapter 9. MARC is at the centre of one of the outstanding British co-operative ventures, the Birmingham Libraries Co-operative Mechanisation Project (BLCMP), the initial co-operating libraries including those of the University of Birmingham, the University of Aston in Birmingham and Birmingham Public Library. One part of this project concerns the production of bookform catalogues and the possibility of union catalogues. The project was initially considered in two articles in *Program* in 1969, one by C F Cayless and R T Kimber, and the other by R M Duchesne (*Program* 3 1969 75-9 and 106-110). Subsequently the project has been well documented, and the latest progress report, 'The Birmingham Libraries' Co-operative Mechanisation Project: progress report, January 1972-June 1973', by D G R Buckle and others, appeared in *Program* 7 (4) October 1973 196-202. Several separate publications which deal with the scheme have also been issued. These include: *Potential use of MARC records in three libraries: report of two surveys carried out for the BLCMP,* by A R Hall, R M Duchesne and S W Massil (London, BNB 1971) and BLCMP *Costing cataloguing systems in three libraries* (Birmingham, BLCMP 1971).

DILS

A commercial service at present being developed which will make use of MARC is DILS (Dataskil Integrated Library System). This is a package system designed to cater for a library's ordering, cataloguing and circulation needs and to provide 'management information' such as various statistics which may be required. The cost of this package is estimated at £5,000 at present, and the users themselves participate in its design and development. The introduction of this service in Great Britain is timely, considering the recent reorganisation of local government. The resultant larger authorities will be more likely, and more able, to computerise. Unlike a system designed for a particular library, DILS must be flexible. No 'ultimate' decisions can be taken and the system must cater for a wide variety of needs. For the technically minded, DILS is a batch and not an on line system, which uses a variable field approach, is designed for a 32K machine, runs on 'George' and is written in Cobol.

Microform catalogues

Another possible method of utilising the output of a computer is to convert it not into book form catalogues but into a microform. In Britain, Buckle and French note upwards of twenty libraries using or experimenting with this method ('The application of microform to manual and machine-readable catalogues' *Program* 6 (3) July 1972 187-203), although there appear to be few developments elsewhere. In America, for instance, only a very limited number of libraries seems to be concerned with the possibilities of microform catalogues. Examples are Los Angeles Public Library and Lockheeds (COM) and New Jersey State Library (microfilmed card). A union catalogue of over one million books in twenty one Louisiana libraries is described in 'Regional numerical union catalog on computer output microfiche' by William E McGrath and Donald Simon in *Journal of library automation* 5 (4) December 1972 217-229.

Kozumplik and Lange focused attention on the possibility of computer produced microfilm catalogues as early as 1967: 'Computer produced microfilm catalog' *American documentation* 18 1967 167-180. This article on the use of COM techniques at Lockheed Missiles and Space Company is updated in 'A COM produced library catalogue' *Information and records management* April/

May 1970 45-6. Developments in COM (Computer Output Micro-film) techniques have since persuaded certain libraries that the use of microfilm as a means of displaying computer formulated catalogues could be advantageous, especially from the point of view of cost. COM is much cheaper than the more normal photo-copying methods of catalogue reproduction.

In the UK, for example, Westminster City Libraries began to use microfilm cassettes for cataloguing purposes in June 1971. Each 'copy' of the catalogue is replaced at monthly intervals with a new updated film of both author and classified sections. The subject index remains in printed form. As the catalogue grows, the intention is to 'spread' the catalogues for public use in the larger lending libraries over several microfilm recorders, so that the enquirer will go to whichever machine holds the sections of the catalogue which he requires. Apart from cost, another advantage of microfilm cassettes is the ability to provide staff catalogues in workrooms at small extra expense and with the minimum loss of space. Larkworthy and Brown ('Library catalogues on microfilm' *Library Association record* 73 (12) December 1971 231-2) maintain that the reaction of the public to this new form has been most encouraging.

Cheshire County Library now has a combined computerised book ordering and cataloguing system, which also involves the pro-duction of adult non-fiction book catalogues on microfilm direct from magnetic tape. This system features on-line (from 0900 to 1700 Monday to Friday) data entry via visual display terminals. Details of this scheme are available in a brochure issued by the County Treasurer in 1972 entitled *Book ordering and cataloguing system*. There is also the article 'Cheshire County Library acquisi-tions and cataloguing system', by S G Berriman and J Pilliner *Program* 7 (1) January 1973 38-59.

A disadvantage of this cataloguing method is that only one person can use a microfilm reader at any one time, and this one person can, therefore, monopolise a complete catalogue (several thousand pages can be held on a single cassette of film). However, this disadvantage can easily be overcome by the provision of multiple readers where necessary. The price of readers is reason-able and the cost of further copies of the film is comparatively negligible.

To sum up, for readers who are not averse to microfilm, and

the modern cassette readers *are* easy to use, this form of catalogue has considerable financial and space saving advantages.

BRIMARC

An interesting experiment is now being undertaken in this field at Brighton. Brighton Public Library feeds in cataloguing data to the BNB and it is there processed and converted by computer into a microfilm catalogue, which is then supplied to the public library ready for use. There is no need for the participating library to concern itself with systems analysis or programming, nor even to have access to a computer. The expansion of this service could be a boon to the smaller college or school library where the cost of computerised bibliographical control is at present prohibitive. The scheme is described by R M Duchesne and L Donbroski 'BNB/ Brighton Public Libraries catalogue project—"BRIMARC"' *Program* 7 (4) October 1973 205-224, and an OSTI report is also available: *BNB/Brighton Public Libraries catalogue project (BRIMARC) report* (London, BNB and Brighton Public Libraries 1973).

Certain elements of the BRIMARC scheme have proved useful in the LASER project (see p 131), which involves the conversion of a regional union catalogue into machine readable form. COM techniques allow the project to utilise centrally produced MARC records (see p 129) for the creation of local systems catalogues.

The computer as the catalogue

A possibility which must be considered is that of using the computer *as the catalogue,* with access via a terminal or VDU (visual display unit). Much progress in this sphere has been made at the Ohio College Library Center, where extensive files are held in the computer, and an on-line computerised shared-cataloguing service is provided for most of the libraries in Ohio. Subject access via the computer will not, however, be available for several years. This system has a three-fold purpose:

1 To provide a union catalogue covering the holdings of member libraries. This is a computer based catalogue and each member has access to it via a cathode ray tube terminal.

2 To provide cataloguing copy for member libraries at low cost. MARC tapes form the basis of the data bank and items can be found by using a card number index, an author-title index or a title index. If there is no exact cataloguing copy in the bank, copy

for a similar item can be displayed on the visual terminal and member libraries can alter the material displayed on the screen so that it matches the book in hand. If similar copy is not available within the MARC based bank, then a member library can do original cataloguing on the cathode ray tube terminal and this information can then be made available, within seconds, to the next library needing copy for that particular title.

3 To produce catalogue cards for all members.

The Ohio system offers some exciting prospects and it has been well covered in the professional press. Dan L Kniesner and Betty J Meyer report on the progress made in 'On-line computer techniques in shared cataloguing' *Library resources and technical services* 17 (2) Spring 1973 225-230. The development and implementation of the system is also described in 'The shared cataloguing system of the Ohio College Library Center', by Frederick Kilgour and others *Journal of library automation* 5 (3) September 1972 157-183.

'Traditional' forms of catalogue

Before the advent of the computer made possible a return to the book catalogue, one of several physical forms could be used to overcome the disadvantages, *eg* lack of flexibility and currency, of the book form.

The guard-book catalogue

In this the entries are made on slips of paper and mounted in the required sequence on the blank leaves of large guard-books, which are like large scrap books in which additional slips of linen or paper on the inner margin allow extra pages to be inserted. The entries have to be kept as widely spaced as possible to allow for additional insertions and, upon the inevitable filling up of a page, the leaf must be removed, the entries cut up and dispersed over an increased number of leaves.

Features: Retains the format of the book catalogue (although it is very much less compact) and permits insertion of entries (albeit with some effort) and updating of the sequence.

Problems: The size, number and bulk of the guard-books. The difficulty of maintaining strict order and the length of time taken when cutting up and remounting is required. The constant withdrawals required by most libraries would make this form impracticable for their purposes.

The BM provides a noteworthy example of this form, running to more than twelve hundred volumes (*cf* the printed catalogue in 263 volumes). Some academic libraries still use it.

The card catalogue

In this each entry is recorded on a separate card of standard size (12·5 cm × 7·5 cm) and the cards are filed in drawers housed in catalogue cabinets.

Features: The arrangement permits complete flexibility and maximum ease of insertion of new entries, and withdrawal of others, so that the catalogue can be completely up to date. It has (theoretically) an infinite capability for expansion. It can be fairly easily guided. Cards are reasonably durable and production of entries on them by typewriting or duplication is not unduly expensive. The physical 'spread' of the catalogue (although this can be a problem) permits consultation by many readers at once.

Problems: The card form is not thought to be as readily acceptable to all library users as, say, the book form, although the force of this argument has been diminished through the years as the form became widely adopted in libraries. The ability of one reader (in spite of the 'spread' mentioned above) physically to monopolise a whole drawer or section of the cabinet causes problems in busy libraries. The possibility of removal and destruction of the cards (although in most cases they are held by rods) by errant users can create a difficulty. But probably the biggest problem of all, which is increasingly being brought home to the very large libraries, is the sheer bulk and remorseless growth of the card form. While it proves an excellent instrument in respect of a reasonably sized library it can become a massive space-eater' in a very large library. A dramatic example of this might be found merely in the title of the following article: F Whitehouse 'NYPL's nightmarish problem: eight million index cards' *Antiquarian bookman* 38 (42) July 1966 4-11.

J H Shera 'The book catalog and the scholar: a re-examination of an old partnership' *Library resources* 6 (3) Summer 1962 210-216 states that the card catalogue 'has reached the point of diminishing returns' and discusses the possible return of the book catalogue produced by non-conventional printing methods. In the same periodical and issue, p 217-222. M R McDonald 'Book catalogs and card catalogs' echoes this theme—'the card catalogue is doomed to destroy itself'—offering the solution of the book catalogue supplemented by card catalogues.

Nevertheless, it should be remembered that the card catalogue is still by far the most popular physical form. Not everyone is convinced that the computer is the answer to every library's problems. Ellsworth Mason in 'Computers in libraries' *Library resources and technical services* 16 (1) Winter 1972 5-10 considers library automation to be 'the backside of brainlessness' and maintains that 'only the reckless waste of money on computerised systems that cost more to do the same thing'. In America 'many are coming to believe that a computer produced book catalogue has little to recommend it over a conventional card catalogue. Because it is not financially possible at present to have an on-line catalogue containing all the data now on library cards and allowing access to all points at which a card catalogue can be consulted, the direction in which libraries may move is towards a single entry manual file. on cards or computer produced microfilm, containing the full bibliographic data and carrying the bibliographic function of the catalogue, but with the finding function automated using drastically reduced bibliographic information': J McRee Elrod 'Years work in cataloguing and classification' *Library resources and technical services* 17 (2) Spring 1973 175-200.

It should be remembered, as previously noted, for example, with regard to the Douglas Aircraft Company and the Ohio College Library Center, that the computer can be utilised to automate the production of catalogue cards. In Great Britain, the University of Liverpool has adopted such an approach. In this case, computer output in punch tape form is run through tape typewriters to produce catalogue cards in an appropriate format.

The sheaf catalogue

In this each entry is recorded on separate paper slips which are filed in specially made loose-leaf binders.

Features: This form is claimed to combine the convenience and 'psychological advantages' of the book-form with the flexibility for insertion and withdrawal of entries of the card catalogue. The entries on paper slips are cheaper to produce than card entries, and can also be reproduced cheaply by carbon copies. Since slips are usually larger than the standard card more space

37

is available for copy and this has led to their use in regional union catalogues, where the entry has to carry a large grid. It occupies less space than the card cabinets.

Problems: While capability for insertion and withdrawal of entries is certainly present, the nature of the binding mechanism on the sheaf holder (screws, springs etc) and the flimsiness of the paper slips make the operations of insertion and withdrawal of entries less convenient. In spite of the ' book form ', with one entry per page, ' sequential scanning ' is not all that easy, although it may be slightly easier than in the card catalogue. The larger area for the entry gives no distinct advantage unless, as noted above, it is to be used for a grid, or perhaps for annotation. Guiding is not very satisfactory.

Some of the larger libraries in Britain, *eg* Liverpool City Libraries, as well as the regional bureaux, have used and are using sheaf catalogues, but there has never been evidence of distinct advantages of the form over the practically universal card catalogue sufficient to oust the latter from its supremacy.

The visible index

Office equipment manufacturers have, in recent years, produced a wide variety of sophisticated devices for the indexing and posting of information, which are in direct line of descent from the card file developed for the library catalogue. Visible indexes, whether in the form of narrow strips mounted in a frame, or metal trays holding cards held flat, hinged and so arranged that a projecting edge is available for a heading, provide the same facility for easy interpolation of new entries.

Wilfrid Plumbe produced stripdex visible indexes for the libraries of various universities in Asia and Africa and has written two useful articles: 'The "stripdex" catalogue' *Library Association record* 64 (4) April 1962 128-131 and 'Another appraisal of the stripdex catalogue' *Library review* 21 (5) Spring 1968 234-236. Some of the points made by Plumbe are queried by Peter Stephen in 'The stripdex catalogue' *Library review* 21 (3) Autumn 1967 137-139. 'The use of visible indexes in the House of Commons Library' is described by D J Englefield in *Library world* 72 (848) February 1971 231-236.

D E Davinson *Periodicals: a manual of practice* (London, Deutsch 2nd ed 1964) p 59-64 indicates the value of visible indexes

for periodicals acquisition and the use of visible indexes for the
indexing and listing of certain categories of material such as
gramophone records, illustrations collections etc, where perhaps
title entry may be brief but descriptive detail may require the
space available on an eight by five or six by four card, is fairly
obvious. Many libraries have found that by photocopying the
strips or the projecting edges of the visible index cards, they have
been able to reproduce usable brief check lists of the materials
listed thereon.

READINGS

Bakewell Ch 10.	Each of these chapters is concerned with
Horner Ch 25.	physical forms of catalogues and provides
Needham Ch 18.	basic reading on the subject.

Scott, A D: *Report on the catalogue use survey: physical forms
and guiding* (Brighton Polytechnic School of Librarianship 1973).
A survey of users' attitudes towards different physical forms of
catalogues. The card catalogue was found to be by far the most
popular followed, in order of popularity, by sheaf, computer produced and microfilm. See also *New library world* 75 (884) February 1974 31-32.

Tauber, M F, *Cataloguing and classification* volume one, part
one of *State of the library art* edited by R R Shaw (New Brunswick, Rutgers University Press, 1960). An interesting table of the
comparative features of various forms of catalogues by C D Gull
is reproduced on pages 69-71, and 'The sheaf catalogue' is discussed on pages 111-116.

Out of the Bath mini-catalogue project (see p 30) has grown the
Bath University Comparative Catalogue Study. One major aim of
this project is to ascertain which form (card, printout, COM roll
film and COM fiche) and order (name, classified, title and KWOC)—
a) best meets demands on the catalogue, b) is easiest to use,
c) is most cost effective. Some interim results are given in 'You
need long nails' by Philip Bryant and Angela Needham *Catalogue and index* (33) Spring 1974 1 and 11-12. Users apparently
castigated the card catalogue but praised the fiche. This contrasts
with the results obtained at Brighton.

Where the automation of library processes is concerned, there
are obviously many more relevant items available than those that
have been cited throughout this chapter.

Some useful general works are:

Cox, Nigel S M and Grose, Michael W ed: *Organisation and handling of bibliographic records by computer* (Newcastle, Oriel Press: Hamden, Conn, Archon 1967). Contains articles by leading experts from Britain and North America.

Dolby, J L, Forsyth, V J and Resnikoff, H L: *Computerised library catalogs: their growth, cost and utility* (Cambridge (Mass), MIT Press 1969). A 'complete feasibility study'—*wrapper.*

Eyre, John and Tonks, Peter: *Computers and systems: an introduction for librarians* (London, Bingley: Hamden, Conn, Linnet 1971).

Henderson, James W and Rosenthal, Joseph A: *Library catalogs: their preservation and maintenance by photographic and automated techniques: a study by the Research Libraries of the New York Public Library* ... (Cambridge (Mass), MIT Press for the New York Public Library, Astor, Lenox and Tilden Foundations 1968).

Higham, Norman: *Computer needs for university library operations* (London, Standing Conference of National and University Libraries 1973). Norman Roberts of Sheffield University has described this report, which is based on an investigation carried out by David Buckle, as a 'best buy'. Actual and proposed computer applications are described and there is a chapter on costs.

Smith, Gloria L and Meyer, Robert S ed: *Library use of computers: an introduction* (New York, Special Libraries Association, 1969).

The Winter 1973 issue (no 32) of *Catalogue and index* includes articles on 'Cornwall's automated cataloguing system', 'MARC at Liverpool University' and the 'Oxford City Libraries computer system'. Salop (*ie* Shropshire) County Library have recently (1974) reissued *An automated stock control system,* by A J Crowe and H I Hammond. This county's catalogues are on microfiche. The use of 'Computers in the regional library bureaux' of the UK is discussed by Ross Bourne in the *Library Association record* 75 (12) December 1973 238-241.

A useful guide to information on computers and libraries:

Tinker, Lynne: *An annotated bibliography of library automation, 1968-1972* (London, Aslib 1973). This contains 445 annotated references.

CHAPTER FOUR

INNER FORMS OF CATALOGUES

A catalogue is, by definition, a list of books in a library or collection, the entries in the list being arranged in some systematic
order. This order, or mode of arrangement, determines the ' inner
form ' of the catalogue.

The author catalogue

The *author catalogue* is a catalogue with, in the main, authors'
names in the headings, arranged alphabetically. The entries will,
however, usually include those for editors, translators, etc. Added
entries for titles are often included in this sequence* so that, most
usually, the form of catalogue should be designated as an *author/
title catalogue*. Identification of a book or document by means of
named author is such an obvious and traditional approach by
users of libraries, that there is little dispute about the primacy and
importance accorded to the author catalogue as a form, and it
still remains the chief object of attention in the catalogue codes.
While some libraries manage to get along without a subject catalogue (or with only a very imperfect version of one), none can
properly afford to dispense with the author or author/title approach.

It should be noted that an author need not necessarily be a
person but can be a *corporate body, ie* some organisation or group
of persons identified by a name and that acts or may act as an
entity.

Bakewell (chapter 4), *Horner* (chapter 4) and *Needham* (chapters 4 and 5) all provide basic reading on the problems of the
author catalogue.

The subject catalogue

The description *subject catalogue* may be given to any catalogue in which the headings on the entries designate the subject

* AACR makes title entry mandatory for most works.

matter of the work and the entries are arranged systematically for subject identification and retrieval. If the headings are words, terms or phrases and are arranged alphabetically, the catalogue is an *alphabetical subject catalogue.* If such subject headings are selected to indicate as precisely as possible the ' specific subject' of the book or document and are linked with connective references between related subjects, the catalogue may be described as an *alphabetico-specific* or *alphabetico-direct catalogue.* If the headings are classification symbols arranged in accordance with the sequence of the classification scheme (preferably complemented with an alphabetical index of subjects), the catalogue is then a *classified subject catalogue.*

Subject cataloguing is extensively covered in the standard cataloguing textbooks: *Bakewell* (chapter 5), *Horner* (section III) and *Needham* (part 2), as well as in works such as *Coates* and *Foskett.*

A subject catalogue which has been claimed to represent a compromise between the alphabetico-direct and the classified forms is the *alphabetico-classed,* in which the entry words of headings consist of selected broad class terms or generic subjects. The subject specification is cited in the accompanying subheading, *eg*

    ARCHITECTURE—Churches
              —Houses
              —Schools

Arrangement throughout is alphabetical. The alphabetico-classed catalogue cannot be accepted as a viable form for contemporary use, having more or less vanished in the nineteenth century. Admittedly it brings together related aspects of subjects, but how are the main headings to be chosen and what steps of division are to be included? The BM *Subject index* has been frequently cited as an example by some writers, but *Jolley* p 109-110 and *Bakewell* p 92 show that no such pattern was in the mind of the original compiler, G K Fortescue. (R Bancroft 'The British Museum subject index' *Indexer* 3 (1) Spring 1962 4-9 attempts to explain BM practice, stating that the arrangement is alphabetical by subjects, *some* of which are subdivided.)

The name catalogue

A variant form of catalogue, whose use has been more or less confined to Britain, is the *name catalogue.* The headings on the entries are those of proper names of persons and places and include both works ' by ' and works ' about ', the entries being arranged in one alphabetical sequence. Some versions are restricted to personal names only. It amounts to an author/title catalogue with that part of an alphabetical subject catalogue relating to proper names added, thus providing partial subject coverage. The value of varying versions of this form of catalogue, which has sometimes been used in conjunction with a classified subject file (in lieu of an alphabetical subject index), has not been satisfactorily proved. *Bakewell* (chapter 6) deals with the name catalogue at some length and provides several case studies of its use.

The dictionary and classified catalogues

The provision of the author/title catalogue form in conjunction with two of the subject catalogue forms (alphabetico-direct in the one case and classified in the other) produces the two 'classical' inner forms of full library catalogue. These are:

1 The *dictionary catalogue,* which inter-files its author/title headings, specific verbal subject headings and connective references in one alphabetical sequence.

2 The *classified catalogue,* in which the principal component is the classified file of subject entries, complemented by alphabetically-arranged indexes of subjects, authors, titles. These indexes may be arranged in a single, or in separate, alphabetical sequence and the author/title index may be a full author/title catalogue or may be more restricted in bibliographical detail than the full entry in the classified file.

Of the two forms, the classified catalogue has the longer history, probably deriving from the original ' inventory ' function of the catalogue whereby, as the books in the old libraries were grouped in broad categories of knowledge and press-marked, the inventory of the book store consequently followed some systematic order of knowledge, however crude. The pattern of systematic arrangement of entries in accordance with a classified order of knowledge became and remains a strong tradition in the libraries (and subject bibliographies) of Europe and Britain to the present day, and although the early shelf-lists would have lacked the complex notation, added entries, and indexes, of the present-day catalogues, they provided the basis for such later developments.

43

The dictionary catalogue came on the scene much later, and emerged in the United States towards the end of the nineteenth century. Alphabetical subject indexes of a sort had been produced in Europe, but the headings were usually limited to words selected from the book title (catchwords, or keywords) and the codified practice of establishing a specific subject heading in words not necessarily derived from the title-page, had to wait for Cutter's *Rules* of 1876. After Cutter, the dictionary catalogue became the almost universally accepted form of catalogue in the American scene and, indeed, was introduced widely elsewhere. The classified catalogue was ousted almost entirely in the United States, but the new method was not so completely accepted in Europe where both forms co-exist today.

The existence of these two forms of subject catalogue has provided a continuing debate among librarians on the relative merits and shortcomings of each form. It is perhaps a tribute to the qualities of *both* forms (if not merely to the conservatism of cataloguers) that, with so much analysis and appraisal being directed at the comparison over such a long period, and with so many librarians with strongly-held convictions participating in the debate, that the situation has remained so little changed throughout the years.

The sections on the dictionary catalogue and the classified catalogue in chapter twenty five of *Sharp* give an historical account of catalogues representative of each form, while John Metcalf in *Subject . . . (op cit)* p 38-43 gives a somewhat opinionated explanation of the history of the divergence in subject catalogue form throughout the library world. Both *Bakewell* (chaper 2, 'History of cataloguing and catalogues' and p 71 and 82) and *Horner* chapter 12 'Historical outline of the subject approach' also provide brief historical accounts. J. McRee Elrod 'The classed catalog in the fifties' *Library resources* 5 (2) Spring 1961, 141-156 reviews attitudes to the classified form on a continental basis, indicating its supremacy in Europe and stating that there are indications in the USA of a willingness to study this form.

The classified catalogue and subject indexing

The use of the notation of the classification scheme in the headings to arrange the subject entries produces a systematic array and logical collocation of subjects derived from the schedules of the chosen scheme. Approach to the subject file can be made directly if the notation for the required subject is known by the user, but most usually, the approach must be made via an alphabetical subject index which should translate the terms of the subject sought into a class number.

Melvil Dewey's 'Relative index', by introducing the practice of qualifying any index term sought by such terms as were indicative of any phase or aspect of it in the classification schedules, laid the foundations of modern subject indexing. He realised that the classification schedules often must separate, quite logically, related topics under different generic classes, and that it should be the function of an index to collect such distributed relatives under the sought term.

Chain procedure

Ranganathan developed this practice further with his 'chain procedure', which systematises the method of preparing subject index entries for the classified catalogue by analysing each component part of the chosen class mark into a series of terms describing the specific subject, and the successive containing classes from which it descends in the classification hierarchy. Each term in the 'chain' thus obtained, successively produces an index entry, qualified if necessary by one or more of the containing terms to indicate the context.

A simple example of chain indexing (using Ranganathan's *Colon classification*) would be:

Subject: The harvesting of the apple
Classification no: J371:7

Chain	J	Agriculture
	J3	Food
	J37	Fruit
	J371	Apple
	J371:7	Harvesting

Index entries:	Harvesting: Apples: Agriculture	J371:1
	Apples: Agriculture	J371
	Fruit: Agriculture	J37
	Food: Agriculture	J3
	Agriculture	J

The fact that chain procedure is dependent upon a classification scheme does present problems in relation to terminology, hierarchical 'faults' in the chain, etc. It cannot be said to be a 'mechanical' but rather a 'semi-mechanical' process and the indexer must use a certain amount of common sense.

Ranganathan had first mooted this method as early as 1938 in his *Theory of library catalogue* (subsequently developing it in later editions of his *Classified catalogue code*) but it was not until the publication of B I Palmer and A J Wells *The fundamentals of library classification* (London, Allen and Unwin, 1951) and more particularly, with the introduction of chain indexing into the *British national bibliography* in 1950—that the method became widely known and accepted in Britain. There is no doubt of the profound effect it has had since upon the theory and practice of the classified catalogue in Britain and, to some extent, abroad. The success with with which BNB, over twenty one years, applied this subject indexing method and other devices such as ' feature headings ' to a huge national bibliography arranged in the form of a classified catalogue, has produced fresh appraisals of the effectiveness of this form of subject catalogue and caused even its most severe critics to look at it again. A basic account of chain indexing is J Mills ' Chain indexing and the classified catalogue ' *Library Association record* (57) 4 April 1955 141-8, while *Coates* gives an account of chain indexing in BNB in the chapter on 'Chain procedure applied to the decimal classification' p 119-131. Further accounts, including details of how chain procedure (as distinct from chain *indexing*) may be used in the construction of subject headings and references for the dictionary catalogue can be found in *Bakewell* (p 84-9) and *Horner* (p 165-184). A programmed guide to chain indexing is also available: T D Wilson *An introduction to chain indexing* (London, Bingley 1971).

The features of the classified catalogue

1 Arrangement of subjects in the classified file is logical and systematic. Co-ordinate and subordinate relationships of subjects are displayed within the framework of the classification schedule providing for a systematic survey of related subject areas.

2 Subject index complements the classified file by collecting under the sought term all aspects of the subject including those which have been logically separated in the classification scheme. Such an index can aid in the formulation and clarification of the subject search.

3 The notation used to arrange the subject file provides a language independent of natural language, free from many of its difficulties, and more accessible to users on a multilingual basis.

4 Subject index provides for flexibility of additions, corrections, and revisions of subject terms with minimum of effort and no dislocation of subject file. Synonymous terms may be directly indexed to class number and referencing may be minimal.

Criticisms that can be made include:

1 Classified file of subject entries reflects any illogicalities present in the classification scheme. Again, with the advance of knowledge, parts of the schedules may go out of date, necessitating revision of the relevant part of the subject catalogue.

2 The notation in the headings of the classified file is not as readily acceptable and comprehensible to the average user as verbal subject headings.

3 Approach to the required subject entries must, in most cases, be an indirect two-step process, because of the need to use the alphabetical index.

4 User does not always require the complete classified sequence of associated subjects, but, quite often, simply wants material on a specific subject quickly.

The dictionary catalogue and subject headings

The alphabetico-specific subject catalogue, which is a basic component of the dictionary catalogue, aims at establishing a verbal subject heading which will be exactly descriptive of the content of the document identified. Cutter's basic rule 161 ' enter a work under its subject heading, not under the heading of a class which includes that subject ' states in these simple terms the basis of dictionary catalogue practice. If natural language permitted the establishment of headings for all possible subjects in uncomplicated and unambiguous terms, or brief phrases, without possibility of conflict between cataloguer and catalogue user, the task would be a simple one.

However, Cutter saw many of the problems that immediately arise, *eg* complex topics stated in lengthy phrases that have yet no brief ' established ' name; compound or overlapping subjects; synonyms; conflict between topic and locality; and he gave the best directions he could conceive towards their solution, such as advocating direct entry (without inversion of terms) under the most commonly accepted name for a subject. He also laid down the basis of the ' syndetic ' structure of the catalogue, by directing that references should be made downwards from generic or containing classes and collaterally from co-ordinate subjects, and by this method the subject catalogue claims to connect inter-related subjects logically, and facilitate a subject search independently of any classification.

Library of Congress *and* Sears' lists of subject headings

US dictionary catalogue practice is still largely based on Cutter's precepts, and the Library of Congress *Subject headings* and Sears' *List of subject headings* (which derives from it), as working tools for subject heading practice, reflect his rules. Sears' list is intended for small and medium size libraries and, on this ground. omits many specific headings which the LC list requires, but *both* lists of headings and recommended references reflect many of the inconsistencies that have grown up through the years as a result of difficulties which Cutter was unable to resolve.

D J Haykin *Subject headings: a practical guide* (Washington, Library of Congress, 1957) attempts to state the principles upon which the LC list operates but *Coates* p 66 remarks 'Little or no attempt has been made to keep theory abreast of the developing practice, with the result that the present day LC *Subject headings* appears to embody a large number of purely arbitrary decisions . . . which do not form anything approaching an overall pattern of practice'. Confirmation of this particular criticism can be found from a somewhat unexpected source, a writer who has continually expounded on the virtues of verbal subject headings. J Metcalfe *Alphabetical . . .(op cit)* states (p 18) that Cutter's *Rules for a dictionary catalog* is the only generally known or recognised code but there has been no edition or revision since 1904 and they do 'not meet the need of sixty years later . . . for good and ill they are no longer strictly followed. The basis of present practice of alphabetico-specific entry is mainly a vague understanding of its basic concept'. A comparison of the two lists of subject headings was reported by Sydney L Jackson 'Sears and LC *subject headings*: a sample comparison' *Library journal* 86 (4) February 1961 755-756, 775 in which it was concluded that the more specific subject headings omitted by Sears would not prove to be disruptive if used in the catalogues of smaller libraries. M F Tauber 'Subject headings and codes' *Library resources* 3 (2) Spring 1959 97-102 suggested the need for a national subject headings code to supplement Cutter's rules and indicated that a study of basic principles was a necessary preliminary.

The latest edition of *Subject headings used in the dictionary catalogs of the Library of Congress* (seventh edition 1966)* has been most efficiently produced by the combination of computer processing, automatic photocomposition and offset process, and as a result of the automated printing techniques developed, it is promised that subsequent new editions will be more up-to-date and more quickly produced than ever before. But there are some indications that the *nature* of the product should be looked into more closely and perhaps subjected to similar systematic analysis. S L Jackson 'Long files under LC subject headings, and the LC classification' *Library resources and technical services* 11 (2) Spring 1967 243-245 cites some LC subject headings which are not subdivided (selected from LC *Catalog: books: subjects.* 1950-1959 and states that, under such headings, many library catalogues will have long files (upwards of 200 entries) in a single author-alphabet, discouraging to the searcher. He suggests that this condition obtains ' partly because the Library of Congress classification frequently affords more specific subject approaches to the material than its subject headings are capable of '. He indicates the need for such headings to be refined by LC, or for the particular libraries to subdivide such accumulations on the basis of the LC class numbers on the entries filed under these headings. The writer concludes ' Two things are reasonably clear: subject files exceeding two hundred entries in a single author-alphabet are dubious assets, and the prospective automating of cataloguing from LC copy will not of itself solve the problem '.

Perhaps the most curious feature of the US subject cataloguing scene (especially as the Library of Congress is fast becoming the automated bibliographic centre of the world) has been the bland, almost complacent, acceptance of the fact that the verbal subject headings presented in LC and Sears lists, from thence being employed in the dictionary catalogues of countless libraries, rest upon no body of logical and consistently-applied principles. This situation is well-described in the section on 'Subject headings' of the article by P S Dunkin 'Cataloguing and CCS: 1957-1966' *Library*

---

* The eighth edition is scheduled for publication late in 1974.

49

resources and technical services 11 (3) Summer 1967 267-288, and a few random quotations from this summary of nine years developments may illustrate the point. 'Both lists (LC and Sears) still suffer from our preoccupation with the "convenience of the public" inherited from Cutter . . . Haykin's work was only an attempt to arrange inherited practice into a logical system . . . specificity is a magic word which we all accept but seldom really define . . . John Metcalfe's *Alphabetical subject indication of information (1965)* is incoherent but stimulating . . . as the ten years ended, Richard Angell was appointed Chief of the newly created Technical Processes Research Office in LC. Perhaps LC will do some re-thinking of subject heading theory.' Angell has in fact now provided a review of the LC list with suggestions for future reorganisation: 'Library of Congress subject headings—review and forecast' in *Subject retrieval in the seventies: proceedings of an international symposium, University of Maryland, May 14-15, 1971*; edited by H Wellisch and T D Wilson (Westport (Conn), Greenwood and University of Maryland School of Library and Information Services; London, Bingley 1972 143-163).

One outspoken critic of LC subject headings is Sanford Berman who, in an article entitled 'Children, "idiots", the "underground" and others' *Library journal* 96 (22) 15 December 1971 4162-4167, considers various headings that illustrate 'the humanity-degrading -intellect-constricting rubbish that litters the LC list'. Berman follows up this article with a book: *Prejudices and antipathies: a tract on the LC subject heads concerning people* (Metuchen (NJ), Scarecrow 1971).

A useful complementary work to the LC list has recently been published, *Classified Library of Congress subject headings*; edited by James G Williams, Martha L Manheimer and Jay E Daily (New York, Dekker 1972) provides, in volume 1, a list of classification numbers in classification order together with the corresponding subject headings—with subheadings and sub-subheadings —that appear bearing those numbers in the 7th edition of the LC list. Volume 2 consists of an alphabetical listing of the subject headings contained in volume 1, with their respective class numbers. It is claimed that it is now possible to locate a general category in the alphabetical list, find this category in the classified list, and then, easily choose an exact subject heading for the book to be catalogued.

Kaiser and Coates

J Kaiser in his *Systematic indexing* (London, Pitman, 1911) has been recognised as having made a significant contribution to the theory of subject headings, even though his approach was from the viewpoint of information indexing rather than book and document cataloguing. He proposed a procedure for breaking down subjects into two elements, ' concretes ' and ' processes '; systematically trying to formulate headings as ' things ', ' places ', etc (the concretes) qualified by ' actions ', ' activities ' (the processes) expressed, or implicit in the concept. Metcalfe *Subject . . . (op cit)* p 297-300 devotes an appendix to a description of Kaiser's work and theories. A paper by Kaiser on his systematic indexing given at a 1926 ASLIB conference is reprinted in *Olding.*

Coates not only analyses the approach of Cutter, Kaiser and others to the problem of verbal headings (chapters 4 and 5, p 31-49) but also develops his own theory for the formulation of headings for compound subjects on a 'significance order' of thing-material-action. He examines the relationship between the elements in some twenty compound subject 'conditions' and, on the basis of his theory, gives a table of relationships, establishing a logical order of the components for the composition of the subject heading. Coates' work is important, not only as a penetrating analysis of the structure of the alphabetical subject catalogue and the problems of subject specification, but also because, as editor of *British technology index* (1962-) he has been able to translate his theories into practice in the headings created therein. The indexing method used in *British technology index,* as well as other various indexing methods and their associated problems, are discussed by Coates in ' Scientific and technical indexing ' *Indexer* 5 (1) Spring 1966 27-34. The production of *British technology index* is now computerised, and the method used is described by Coates in 'Computerization of *British technology index*: man-machine collaboration in the production of indexes' *Inspel* 3 (3/4) October 1968 147-163.

The features of the dictionary catalogue

1 A single sequence of author/title/subject headings in alphabetical order is easily comprehensible to the user since it reflects the pattern established by dictionaries, encyclopedias, etc.

2 The single sequence permits ease of consultation, while the specific heading facilitates quick reference. The 'syndetic' chain of subject references gives 'lead-through' from generic to specific subjects and from collateral subjects.

3 The subject headings are independent of any classification scheme used, and thus there is freedom to establish headings which will collect related material which has been separated in various classes in the classification schedules.

4 Subject headings can be shaped to match the user's terminology.

Criticisms that can be made include:

1 Verbal subject headings also separate related classes and subjects and 'scatter' them through the array of catalogue entries on the basis of their accidental occurrence in the alphabet.

2 The network of references and cross-references can be often bewildering to the user.

3 Dependence upon a list of 'established' subject headings leads to difficulties with semantic change and obsolescence of terms.

4 The allegedly simple alphabetical sequence of author-title and subject headings can become extremely complex as the catalogue grows and can lead to difficulties in both filing and retrieval.

The divided catalogue

This latter difficulty has resulted in certain US academic and other large libraries 'dividing' their catalogues into separate author/title and alphabetical subject sequences on the grounds of relieving congestion, lessening complex filing problems, increasing ease of consultation and producing a better physical layout for the catalogue. This step, however, is a fairly fundamental reversal of the principle of the classic form of the dictionary catalogue and does not seem to meet with universal approval. The chapter on 'The divided catalog' p 92-101 in M F Tauber *Cataloging and classification* (volume one, part one of *State of the library art*—New Brunswick, Rutgers University Press, 1960) gives a concise summation of the US position on this matter. (The chapters in the same work on 'The dictionary catalog' p 65-67 and 'The classified catalog' p 78-91 provide a useful summary of opinion on these forms derived from the literature up to the late nineteen fifties, while part 2 of the volume (Carlyle J Frarey *Subject headings*) is devoted to a wide-ranging review of developments in this area.) James Wilson McGregor 'In defense of the dictionary catalog' *Library resources and technical services* 15 (1) Winter 1971 28-33 maintains that the dictionary catalogue has distinct advantages over the divided catalogue. The latter can *increase* congestion and confusion and necessitate the duplication of cross references. The 'congestion' problem is further investigated in 'Congestion at card and book catalogs—a queuing theory approach', by Abraham Bookstein *Library quarterly* 42 (3) July 1972 316-328. *Bakewell* (p 175) considers the main problems of dividing the catalogue as being cost and duplication. The same writer also points out (p 176) that the idea of a divided catalogue is not new: 'users of the classified catalogue have lived with it for years'.

The classified versus the dictionary catalogue

A comprehensive tabulation and comparison of the pros and cons of the classified catalogue and the dictionary catalogue is provided by *Shera and Egan* p 14-21. The basic textbooks (*Bakewell* chapter 5—'The subject catalogue'; *Horner* chapter 9 'The "conventional" dictionary catalogue', *chapter* 10 'The classified catalogue' and *chapter* 11 'The "conventional" dictionary and classified catalogues compared'; and *Needham* chapter 9 'The classified catalogue' and chapter 10 'The alphabetical subject catalogue'), all give brief assessments of each form. *Bakewell* appears to favour the classified catalogue, *Horner* is of the opinion that there is little to choose between the two, whilst *Needham* writes: 'Given a more carefully planned procedure for dealing with subject headings and references, much could certainly be said in favour of the dictionary catalogue, for although it can never be as satisfactory a collocative record as the classified catalogue, it does offer a different subject arrangement from the one found on the shelves'. Sakae Yamashita '[Future of the alphabetical subject catalogue. Japanese]' *Tosh-Kai* 23 (4) November 1971 131-143 favours neither form. He considers subject catalogues to be generally unpopular because of difficulties of compilation and because an adequate substitute can be provided by a shelf list and title catalogue. However, this writer believes that of the two forms, the alphabetical subject catalogue is easier for readers than the classified catalogue, in spite of its separation of related subjects. This statement could, of course, be debated at some length. *Bakewell* points to the problems of terminology and presumes that the rule of specificity is unsatisfactory as it is so frequently broken, that is by such devices as inversion and subdivision. Let the last word belong to *Horner*: 'Insufficient research has been made into the nature of subject enquiries. It is doubtful, anyway, if a generalised conclusion can ever be reached because of the widely varying nature of subject needs and the way they are articulated.'

READINGS

Bakewell
Coates ⎫
Foskett ⎬ All of these provide basic reading. Coates and Foskett are particularly important with regard to subject work.
Horner ⎭
Shera & Egan

Other readings:

Jolley Ch 4 'The subject catalogue'.

Mann, Margaret: *Introduction to cataloguing and the classification of books* (Chicago, ALA 1943). Ch 9 and 10 deal with the dictionary catalogue, subject headings and Sears and LC lists.

Metcalfe, J: *Subject classifying and indexing of libraries and literature* (Sydney, Angus and Robertson 1959) Ch 8 'The classified catalogue' and ch 11 and 12 'The dictionary catalogue' are useful, although the whole work is somewhat marred by the author's commitment to the alphabetical subject catalogue being carried as far as abuse of Ranganathan, BNB, and other theories or practices which conflict with his own views. The same author's *Alphabetical subject indication of information* (New Brunswick, Rutgers University Press 1965) contains much useful information on subject heading theory although it somewhat belies its series title ' Rutgers series on systems for the intellectual organization of information ' in not being a very well organised document.

CHAPTER FIVE

GENERAL HISTORY (2)

At this point it is perhaps opportune, now that an awareness has been gained of what the catalogue does, what it looks like and how it is arranged, to return to our historical studies and consider briefly:

1 The major contributions made by certain individual librarians, national institutions and international organisations.

2 Some actual catalogues which are illustrative of the development of the various inner forms described in the previous chapter.

Panizzi

Sir Anthony Panizzi (1797-1879), Keeper of Printed Books at the British Museum in 1837, later Principal Librarian (1856), was the central figure in the 'battle of the rules' controversy which raged around the deficiency and slowness of production of the British Museum catalogues. With his associates (including J Winter Jones and Edward Edwards) he formulated the first version of the famous 91 rules which were accepted in 1839 and published in 1841. Panizzi's code embodied many of the cataloguing principles upon which other subsequent codes were drawn up and it was widely acclaimed throughout the library world. A full account will be found in chapter ten of *Norris*. The fascinating dialogue between Panizzi and the 'Commissioners appointed to inquire' is reproduced as the first reading, p 5-29 in *Olding*.

Jewett

Charles C Jewett (1816-1868), when librarian of Brown University USA, published an author catalogue to which was appended an alphabetical 'topical index' in 1843. Later, in 1852, as librarian of the Smithsonian Institution, he published a report *On the construction of catalogues of libraries,* in which he set forth the first American rules for author entry and suggested an alphabetical list of subjects as supplementary to the ' general ' catalogue. *Pettee* names Jewett, not Cutter, as 'father of our modern library methods' and points to his influence as far afield as the Liverpool catalogue of 1872.

Crestadoro

Andrea Crestadoro (1808-79) was a reader in the British Museum at the time when there was still great unhappiness about the progress of the cataloguing. In 1856 he issued a pamphlet *The art of making catalogues of libraries* advocating detailed main entries, each entry beginning with the author's name. The main entries needed ' no particular arrangement ', however, but were to be supplemented by an index of names and subjects, essentially alphabetical in arrangement, connected by cross references. He later became the third city librarian of Manchester where the 1864 to 1879 supplementary volumes to the 1864 reference catalogue were arranged according to his theory. Crestadoro, however, suggested that subject headings should be taken from titles, a suggestion strongly disagreed with by Charles A Cutter (1837-1903).

Cutter

Cutter when making the *Catalogue of the library of the Boston Athenaeum* (five volumes 1874-82), not only worked out his systematic dictionary plan therein, but in 1876 published his *Rules for a dictionary catalog*. His rules for author/title entries not only had an obvious influence on the AA code and on subsequent American practice, but those for subject headings, some half dozen pages, have formed the basis of subject heading practice until the present day.

These four librarians typify the achievement of individuals in the nineteenth century formative era of modern cataloguing. In the middle of the 1870's, however, the library associations of the UK and the USA were formed, and corporate agreements in the form of codes of rules (see chapter 6) and the examples and practice demonstrated by the developing catalogues of the large libraries (particularly when their catalogues were published) became more influential than individual voices.

The Library of Congress

The decision of the Library of Congress, upon reorganisation in the period 1899-1901, to choose the dictionary catalogue and to print its cards, so making them available to other libraries, has made it a dominant influence on US cataloguing practice ever since, as evidence by the authority of such publications as *Subject headings used . . .* and *Rules for descriptive cataloging.* (The latter now having provided the basis for the rules for description in the North American text of *Anglo-American cataloging rules, 1967.*

Another major cataloguing development, in which the Library of Congress has played a leading rôle, has been the introduction of project MARC and automated bibliographic services (see also p 129 and 171).

The British Museum

The British Museum Library, whose catalogue entries were never available in the same way as those of LC, did not achieve, or indeed seek, a similar rôle. However, since the 1950s with the BNB cataloguing the books received by copyright deposit in the BM (from 1967 the books received by the agency for the copyright libraries have been used), and providing (since 1956) printed cards for them, there is every indication of the emergence of a similar pattern, especially as both the BNB and the BM are to be part of the new British Library.

The British Library

The decision to form a British Library by bringing together the British Museum Library, the National Central Library, the National Lending Library for Science and Technology, the National Reference Library of Science and Invention and the formerly independent British National Bibliography has been one of the most, if not the most, significant happening in librarianship in the UK in recent years. Is there to be at long last a truly national library and a national cataloguing service? There is much to be done and many questions to be answered. Is it feasible, for instance, to convert the catalogues of the British Museum and other major libraries to machine readable form (see also p 60)? There are great hopes for the British Library: the next few years will reveal whether these hopes are to be realised.

It is imperative that automation be considered for solving many of the problems that will face the British Library and a useful report is: Department of Education and Science *The scope for automatic data processing in the British Library* 2 parts (London,

HMSO 1972). A note dealing with the application of automation to the bibliographic records and processes of the British Library, with the recommendations in the above report, and with subsequent developments appears in *Catalogue and index* (29) Spring 1973 1 and 7-9 ('ADP and the British Library', by Maurice Line).

International Federation of Library Associations

In the international cataloguing field, IFLA has played and is continuing to play a vital rôle. Mention may be made, for instance, of the part played by its Working Group on the Co-ordination of Cataloguing Principles, set up in 1954, from which eventually the International Conference on Cataloguing Principles of 1961 was to blossom. There is also the work of IFLA's various committees, such as the Committee on Uniform Cataloguing Rules. In 1971 IFLA set up its Cataloguing Secretariat, based in London, and at its meeting in Brussels in December, 1973, the IFLA Executive Board took the first steps in implementing its long term programme of universal bibliographical control (UBC). It was decided to set up an International Office for UBC, into which the Cataloguing Secretariat will be merged to provide the nucleus of its professional staff. The British Library will continue to provide support and hospitality for the International Office for UBC, as it has done in the past for the Cataloguing Secretariat.

Certain current projects of IFLA are of considerable interest. These include a survey of existing codes for non-book materials and a survey of cataloguing-in-source (see p 132).

IFLA cataloguing activities and other matters are dealt with in *International cataloguing*, the quarterly bulletin of the IFLA Committee on Cataloguing. In the January/March 1974 issue (3 (1) 5-8) appears a chronology, bibliography and a retrospective view of the IFLA Committee on Cataloguing 1954-1974.

Lubetzky

In the spate of conferences held and codes issued during the twentieth century, only one name has seemed to emerge to anything like the prominence of the earlier cataloguing theorists. Seymour Lubetzky, consultant on bibliographic and cataloguing policy in the Library of Congress, was invited by the ALA to prepare a study of the much criticised 1949 ALA rules. His *Cataloging rules and principles* (Washington, Library of Congress 1953) criticised the code on the grounds of having too numerous rules, with over-lapping, duplication, and inconsistency, and proposed that a revised code should be based more upon general principles, rather than consist of attempted enumeration of all possible difficulties and problems. His critique provided a penetrating analysis of the theory and practice of cataloguing, against which the codification of catalogue rules and the making of catalogues had to be re-examined.

Examples of printed catalogues

Much valuable knowledge of the history of catalogues and cata-loguing can be gained by study of the actual catalogues in their various forms. Below is a selective list of printed catalogues (many of the more recently published being available in larger libraries), which is arranged chronologically in the various categories of 'inner form' of the catalogue.

Author catalogues

The British Museum catalogues provide a conspectus of catalogue history ranging from the two volume catalogue of 1787, the seven volume catalogue of 1813-19, and the catalogues of 1881-1905 (ninety-five volumes with fifteen supplementary volumes). Publi-cation of the catalogue begun in 1931, was suspended in 1954 after fifty-one volumes to letters DEZW had been published. In great contrast to its ill-fated predecessor, the photo-lithographic pub-lication of the *General catalogue of printed books* was signally successful, the entire production being achieved in the space of six years. Covering holdings up to 1955, it commenced publication in 1959 and was completed in October 1966 with a total of 263 volumes containing over four million entries. This was later re-printed by Readex Microprint Ltd. in a compact edition of 27 volumes and at a price which placed it within the financial reach of many smaller libraries. Supplementary volumes listing addi-tions for the years 1963 (five volumes), 1964 (seven volumes), 1965 (six volumes) and a cumulated ten-year supplement for the years 1956-1965 (in approximately fifty volumes containing 700,000 entries) have been published. This is to be followed by further ten yearly supplements. Peter Brown 'GK 3 the end of an era' *Catalogue & index* 1 (5) Jan 1967 pages 1 and 12, briefly recounts the history of the publication of the several British Museum catalogues over the years, concluding by predicting that, with the advent of automation, the era of the highly successful photo-lithography process nevertheless will prove to be short. 'Some problems of maintaining a computer edition of the General Catalogue of Printed Books' are discussed by J W Jolliffe in *Libri* 21 (1-3) 1971 109-117.

The *Catalogue of the London Library* was first issued in 1847. The latest edition of the main catalogue (two volumes 1913-14, with supplementary volumes published in 1920, 1929 and 1953) follows the pattern designed by Sir Charles H Wright. There are separately published subject indexes (four volumes published at intervals 1909-1955). The *John Rylands Library Manchester catalogue of printed books* (three volumes 1899) and the *Edinburgh University Library catalogue of printed books* (three volumes 1918-1923) are representative of their period.

Contrasting examples of the production of author catalogues of great national libraries can be found in 1 the *Catalogue général des livres imprimés* of the Bibliothèque Nationale, which published volume 1 in 1897 and in 1973 was up to the letter v, each volume (of which there are now well over two hundred) representing the acquisitions up to the date of printing of the volume; and 2 *Library of Congress catalog: books: authors* which by photolithography reproduced its printed card entries in page form in 167 volumes covering its holdings up to 1942. Two twenty-four volume supplements brought it up to 1952, and it is continued by the *National union catalog* (which includes author entries contributed by other US research libraries) appearing at monthly, quarterly, annual and five yearly cumulations.

A new and augmented twelve year catalog, being a compilation into one alphabetical sequence of the 4th and 5th supplements to the *National union catalog,* in 125 volumes, was published by Rowman and Littlefield between 1970 and 1972 (*The national union catalog 1956 through 1967*).

Publications of the largest book catalogue ever, the *National union catalog, pre-1956 imprints,* has been undertaken by the Library of Congress. The catalogue will appear in an estimated 610 volumes (of which about half have so far appeared) published over ten years, and contain some sixteen million entries covering the location of ten million titles in 700 North American libraries. The firm which produced the British Museum *General catalogue* were awarded the contract and have issued a volume describing the vast undertaking: *Prospectus for the national union catalog, pre-1956 imprints* (London, Mansell, 1967).

Classified catalogues

Some early examples of the classified catalogue include: *Catalogue of the Signet Library Edinburgh* issued by George Sandy in 1827; *Royal Institution Library catalogue* ' methodically ' arranged with an author index, issued by William Harris in 1809; *Cambridge University, Queen's College Library catalogue* ' methodically ' arranged, issued by Thomas Hartwell Horne in 1827.

The Literary and Philosophical Society of Newcastle-upon-Tyne Library catalogue of 1903 was classified by DC and had author and subject indexes. *Glasgow Public Libraries union catalogue of additions* (six volumes for the period 1929-1955), and *Westminster Public Libraries classified catalogue of non-fiction additions 1952-1964* (see also p 33), are good examples of contemporary printed classified catalogues.

US examples of classified catalogues (printed by photo-reproduction of the existing card catalogues) are *American Geographical Society research catalogue* begun in 1923, published 1962; and *Engineering Societies Library, New York classed subject catalog* begun in 1913 using UDC, published in 1963.

Dictionary catalogues

Early examples are: *Birmingham Reference Library catalogue* issued 1869 by J D Mullins on the ' title-a-line ' basis; *Liverpool Reference Library catalogue* (1872); Cutter's five volume *Boston Athenaeum Library catalog* (1874-82); *Peabody Institute, Baltimore library catalog* (thirteen volumes 1883-1905) with many analytical entries; *Index-catalog of the library of US Surgeon-General's office* begun in 1880 by John Shaw Billings, perhaps the most splendid early example of dictionary cataloguing combined with periodical and analytical indexing (continued after 1950 as *National Library of Medicine catalog*).

Liverpool Public Libraries catalogues of non-fiction added (nine volumes 1925 to 1969) and *Bristol Public Libraries annual catalogues of additions* (last issued 1966) provide two examples of current dictionary catalogues. Bristol have also recently issued

(1962) a five volume dictionary catalogue of non-fiction published prior to 1955 and catalogues of additions 1955-59 (two volumes) and 1960-64 (two volumes).

US examples of dictionary catalogues (photo-reproduced from card catalogues) are *Metropolitan Museum of Art, New York catalog* (twenty five volumes Boston, G K Hall 1960) and *Columbia University School of Library Service dictionary catalog* (six volumes Boston, G K Hall 1962). Any available examples of G K Hall reproductions can be studied with great profit since they reproduce so directly the original catalogue entries.

Subject catalogues

The *Subject index of modern works added to the library of the British Museum* covers the period from 1881 to 1960, although a gap presently exists for the years 1951 to 1955. The six volumes for 1956 to 1960, produced in a larger format, were published out of sequence because ' of a different method of preparing copy '. The BM *Subject index* is an alphabetical subject catalogue with somewhat erratic variations in headings and subdivisions between the quinquennial issues from 1902.

London Library subject index (1909 with three supplementary volumes 1920, 1929, 1953). A detailed alphabetical subject catalogue with certain eccentricities *eg* singular noun often (but not always) preferred in subject headings.

Library of Congress catalog: *books*: *subjects* (1950-1954 twenty volumes; 1955-1959 twenty two volumes). Monthly issues, quarterly, annual and quinquennial cumulation (the 1971 cumulation alone, for example, covered eleven volumes). Begun as a complement to author catalogue and interesting as an example of Congress subject headings in use.

The above three subject catalogues are respectively characterised as ' a conscientious civil servant ' (BM); ' a competent British lady ' (London Library); ' an organization man caught in a tremendous machine ' (LC) in Archer Tayler *General subject-indexes since 1548* (Philadelphia, University of Philadelphia Press, 1966) chapter 7 p 298-304. The book is concerned with subject bibliographies more than subject catalogues of libraries, but the above section, which deals particularly with the history of the compilation of the *London Library subject-index* is worth consultation.

Computer produced printed catalogues

A complete picture can only be gained by a study, in addition to the above, of various computer-produced catalogues beginning, in the UK, for example, with early catalogues such as that of Camden Public Library and following with an examination of later catalogues such as those of Coventry Public Library and Hatfield Polytechnic. Some of the various libraries in both the UK and the USA which have issued or are issuing computer produced printed catalogues are noted in chapter 3.

READINGS

Bakewell Ch 2 'History of cataloguing and catalogues'.

Horner Ch 12 'Historical outline of the subject approach'.

Metcalf (*see* reading list at the end of ch 4). Ch 3 'Catalogues and indexes from past to present'.

Olding The reading on Panizzi has been cited above. The editor's introductory notes and the readings from other writers, particularly Cutter, Osborn and Lubetsky should be noted.

Pettee Ch 2 'History of the dictionary catalog'. Deals particularly with US catalogues.

Pre-conference Institute of Library Automation, *San Francisco, 1967 Library automation: a state of the art review,* edited by Stephen R Salmon (Washington, ALA 1969). Includes sample pages from catalogues produced by computer.

Sharp Ch 25 'History of catalogues'.

Rowland Contains several useful papers, including:

Charlton, Alice 'Cataloging, past and present—comparative notes'.

James, Minnie Stewart Rhodes 'The progress of the modern card catalog principle'.

Martel, Charles 'Cataloging, 1876-1926'.

CHAPTER SIX

DEVELOPMENT OF THE CODES

BM Rules

1841 BRITISH MUSEUM RULES: *Rules for compiling the catalogue of printed books, maps and music in the British Museum* (London, British Museum revised edition 1936).

When originally published in 1841 there were 91 rules. The current edition has 41 rules with additional unnumbered rules in the last two chapters for maps and music. The code was designed for an alphabetical catalogue arranged primarily under authors' names in which only one 'main' entry would carry fairly full bibliographical details with shorter 'added' entries often being preferred to simple cross-references.

Its importance lies not only in the fact of its continuing application to the catalogue of a great national library, but also in its primacy *ie* it was the 'founding code', being the first systematic code of rules drawn up to guide the compiler of an author catalogue. All later codes derived to some extent from it. Again it had immediate influence on the rules of other large libraries such as the Bodleian and Cambridge University and less directly perhaps, but just as importantly, upon the decisions of subsequent code committees.

The features that emerge in contrast to subsequent codes relate principally to works that tend to lack personal names in their authorship. The broad philosophy underlying this matter would appear to be towards avoiding direct title entry except as a last resort, by extracting any element from the title of the work that might be used as a heading, *eg* the sixth and *last* alternative for entry of anonymous work is under first word of title not an article (BM 18f). The concept of 'corporate authorship' (the collective responsibility of an organisation or a named group of persons for the content of a document) first emerged in BM. Another singular feature is the kind of classified element introduced by the use of such form headings for main entries as 'dictionaries, encyclopaedias, directories' etc. Latterly, BM policy has tended towards the gradual removal of such headings (academies and congresses, for instance, have been dispersed, as have entries under the heading 'periodical publications', which was the main entry heading, subdivided by place, for all periodicals not issued by a society or institution).

F C Francis deals concisely with the history and origins of the BM code in *Piggott* (chapter 3) but the current problems facing the BM in its new role as part of the British Library have yet to be resolved. They are analysed in Part 1 of *The British Library and AACR: report of a study commissioned by the Department of Education and Science* (London, Library Association, 1973). The important question is whether a new complete catalogue should be compiled or should the old catalogue be closed and a new one started solely for additions after a certain date? Although the BM has always felt that its readers should have only *one* catalogue to consult, it is admitted that its cataloguing rules are outdated and part 2 of the above report provides a rule-by-rule comparison of the BM code and AACR as interpreted and used by the BNB. The BM, whilst it is prepared to accept many AACR rulings, is still at variance with AACR in some instances (such as surnames with epithets). There is no doubt that the BM recognises the need for change but, at the time of writing, the exact changes cannot be specified.

AA Code

1908 AA CODE: *Cataloguing rules: author and title entries compiled by committees of the Library Association and the American Library Association* (1908).

Variously known as the *Joint code,* the *Anglo-American code,* the AA *Code.* In 1904, the two associations, having previously produced independent codes and being engaged in revising them agreed to co-operate in the production of a joint code which would bring uniformity into the cataloguing practice of the English-speaking countries. Melvil Dewey, a member of the US committee, had written a letter to the LA committee making this proposal in 1900, and the idea was taken up. Four years of deliberation and consultation produced the 1908 *Code.*

The 174 rules relate to the entry, heading and descriptive cataloguing of works for an author and title catalogue ' guided chiefly by the requirements of larger libraries of a scholarly character'.

The prefaces acknowledge, and the notes throughout the text indicate, the influence of Cutter, Linderfelt's eclectic rules, Dziatzko and the *Prussian instructions,* and the BM and LC *Rules.*

Its importance lies in the fact of its being the first international cataloguing code, in the extent of its rapid and widespread adoption and use by all kinds and sizes of libraries in the two countries since its introduction, and in its continued use in Britain (although throughout the fifty-odd years of its use here there has been an ever-growing tendency towards modification and amplification, accelerated by the 1941 and 1949 ALA codes).

How long it will continue to exist in many and various annotated versions in British libraries in view of the publication of the *Anglo-American cataloguing rules, 1967* is a matter for some speculation.

The arrangement was an improvement on preceding codes. The ' Entry and heading section ' (AA 1-135) is divided into personal authors, corporate authors, title entries; the remaining rules (AA 136-174) cover description. Much importance has been attached to the occasions when the two committees failed to agree, but this happened with just eight rules out of 174 and centred principally upon the British (and BM tradition) of preferring the earliest of variant names and titles, while US (and Cutter's) practice tended towards the latest or ' best known '. The sample entries illustrating rules have always been the source of much criticism in that many are in German and Latin. The section on corporate authorship, with its undefined distinction and differential treatment of institutions (under place) and societies (under name), has provided grounds for much conflict throughout the years. A list of definitions of terms precedes the rules, but there is nowhere any statement of principles or purpose, nowadays considered so important.

A good critical assessment of the AA *Code* is to be found in *Needham* (p 40-43) and similar brief accounts in *Bakewell* (p 30-32) and *Horner* (p 66-69). E L J Smith's article 'Anglo-American *Code*' in Landau *Encyclopaedia of librarianship* (third edition London, Bowes 1966) is a concise reading on its origin and development.

Cutter's Rules

1876 CUTTER'S RULES: *Rules for a dictionary catalog* by Charles A Cutter (Washington Government Printing Office, fourth edition 1904).

The first edition (1876) had 205 rules, which were tested by application to the catalogue of the Boston Athenaeum Library, which Cutter compiled. The fourth edition, published in the year after his death, has 369 rules, covering not only rules for author/title entry and description, but also form entry, alphabetical subject entry and the filing of entries. It was and is the most complete set of rules ever produced by an individual, and provided the first extensive codification of cataloguing practice in the form of copious notes on many matters of difficulty, frequently enunciating principles that continue to be studied to the present day.

Its importance lies not only in this latter area but on the influence Cutter's pragmatic approach has had upon American practice, particularly evident in the US alternative rules in the AA code. Cutter emphasised in many ways that the ' convenience of the user should be preferred to the ease of the cataloguer ', and recommendations to use the ' best known ' form of author's name and to follow ' customary use of the names of subjects' reflect this approach. By enunciating the principle of specific subject entry and connective referencing he laid the foundations for all subsequent dictionary catalogue practice. In the principle that the catalogue should not only facilitate the finding of a given book but should also fulfil the other object of showing what the library has under a given author, he reinforced the contention that the catalogue should assemble literary units.

Other features of the code include: rules for corporate authorship more developed and numerous than BM with valuable discussion on the difficulties; provision for short, medium and full cataloguing to suit different styles of catalogues recognised; double entry recommended quite often when no one alternative is completely acceptable. A list of objectives is given at the beginning of the code, followed by comprehensive list of definitions. Rules arranged—ENTRY (where to enter) 1 author catalog 2 title catalog 3 subject catalog 4 form catalog. STYLE (how to enter) covering description and filing arrangement. Rules for cataloguing special materials (MSS, music, maps etc) by other compilers are included at the end of the work.

Concise accounts of Cutter's *Rules* will be found in *Norris* (p 103-6) and *Needham* (p 39-40). Both *Bakewell* and *Horner* also make numerous references to them.

Prussian instructions

1899 THE PRUSSIAN INSTRUCTIONS: *Instruktionen für die alphabetischen Kataloge der preussischen Bibliotheken.* 1899. *2 Ausgabe.* 1908 (Berlin, 1915).

The Prussian instructions; rules for the alphabetical catalogues of the Prussian libraries translated from the second edition by Andrew Osborn (Ann Arbor, 1938).

In 1886, Professor K Dziatzko published his *Instruktionen für die ordnung der Titel im alphabetischen Zettelkatalog der Königlichen und Universitäts-Bibliothek zu Breslau.* This earlier German code formed the basis for the *Prussian instructions* (and was also the framework for K A Linderfelt's *Eclectic card catalogue rules,* 1890, the pioneer work in comparing cataloguing rules, which compared Dziatzko's rules with those of BM, Cutter and other authorities). The *Prussian instructions* were applied with great success to the German *Union catalogue* produced by the Prussian State Library—the *Deutscher Gesamtkatalog*—which drew many libraries in Germany and Austria into conformity with the rules, the philosophy being agreement on essentials, freedom on details. Co-operative cataloguing among German libraries in the earlier part of this century thus became a working reality when it was still little practised elsewhere.

The sections of the rules include: the entry of titles in alphabetical card catalogues; arrangement of titles; arrangement under authors' names; arrangement under real titles; alphabetical arrangement of authors' names and real titles. Appendices include: transliteration scheme; description of incunabula; rules for use of capital letters.

Essential differences to Anglo-American practice are: 1 the non-acceptance of the principle of corporate authorship, entry being made under title and 2 the *grammatical* arrangement of title entries, as compared to Anglo-American practice of natural word order. Andrew Osborn in his article ' Cataloguing and cataloguing codes in other countries today ' *Library quarterly* 25 (4) October 1956 276-285 discusses the code at some length and states ' Three features stand out . . . 1 it is not a theoretical utterance but consists of carefully thought out rules . . . based on practical experience; 2 wording throughout is clear and unambiguous, all terms being defined; 3 the grasp of essentials displayed by its framers is truly noteworthy '.

Brief accounts of the *Prussian instructions* can be found in *Bakewell* (p 29-30) and *Horner* (p 61-63).

The Prussian code was used in a simplified form by some public libraries and in the 1930s a special version was produced for their use. Following the second world war, a revision was issued (1951) which was binding on all public libraries in the GDR. This revision was apparently necessitated by the 'great demand made on public libraries in a socialist state'. With the introduction of open access the catalogue needed to be more informative and further German codes appeared in the mid-1960s. In addition, following the work of IFLA and ICCP, a German language committee on cataloguing rules began work in 1965. The introduction of this new code is discussed in two articles by Ilse Rix entitled 'Einfuhrung neuer Regeln für die alphabetische Katalogisierung und ihre Bedeutung für die staatlichen Allgemeinbibliotheken' [The introduction of new rules for alphabetically arranged catalogues and their significance for state public libraries] *Bibliothekar* 27 (1) January 1973 9-15 and (2) February 1973 85-94. The new code is now in process of publication and a commentary and a comparison with the *Prussian instructions* can be found in 'Eintragungen unter Personen, Korperschaften unt Sachtiteln nach den neuen "Regeln für die alphabetische Katalogisierung" (Teil 1)', by Peter Kittel *Zentrablatt fur Bibliothekswesen* 87 (1) November 1973 650-660.

Vatican code

1931 VATICAN CODE: Biblioteca Apostolica Vaticana: *Norme per il catalogo degli stampati. Terza edizione* (Citta del Vaticano 1949).

Vatican Library: rules for the catalog of printed books translated from the second Italian edition . . . edited by Wyllis E Wright (Chicago, ALA 1948).

The reorganization of the rich resources of the Vatican Library was begun in the 1920's. The Carnegie Endowment for International peace subsidised and collaborated in the project, sending, in 1928, four eminent American librarians, Martel, Hanson, Bishop, Randall, who were assisted by American-trained Vatican librarians, to revise the cataloguing practice of the library. The choice of the dictionary form of catalogue and the subsequent provision of printed cards are evidence of the American influence, while a very valuable product of the Commission was the emergence of the new cataloguing rules.

The basis of the codification was the Italian cataloguing rules of 1911 with the addition of suitable elements of the AA *Code* to ' internationalize ' the Italian rules. However, it was found necessary further to widen the scope of these rules and to provide guidance in the development of subject headings. John Ansteinsson, a Norwegian librarian who had studied in the US, again re-worked the *Rules* after the departure of the other members of the Commission and the resulting code was published by the Vatican in 1931.

The first edition, a work of about 400 pages, contained some 500 rules covering the whole field of author/title entry, description, subject entry and filing. It was quickly accepted by cataloguers in many countries as the best and most complete code then in existence. An expanded second edition was published in 1939. During the thirties and forties the Vatican code was frequently cited as ' the best statement of American cataloguing practice ', 'the most complete code for subject heading work' etc, although the English translation was not available until 1948, by which time the ALA (1949) rules were about to appear.

It has been stated that while the author entry and descriptive cataloguing sections have been less useful and influential than they might have been if translated earlier, nevertheless part 3, ' Subject headings ', is unequalled in any language in its treatment of the fundamental principles of subject entry, and is the most important treatment since Cutter. The subject headings section is divided into two major parts, the first dealing with general principles and form, and the second with application to special areas—history, language, literature, geographical subjects. The subject heading dilemma, first raised by Cutter, of place versus subject is treated, but the compilers submit that frequently only subjective judgement can be the basis of decision.

An informative review of the English translation of the second edition has been provided by J H Shera ' Vatican library: rules for the catalog of printed books ' *Library quarterly* 18 (4) October 1948 299-302.

Horner deals with this code on p 75-76 and 134-135. *Bakewell* mentions it briefly on p 32-33.

ALA rules and LC rules for descriptive cataloguing

1949 ALA RULES: ALA *Cataloguing rules for author and title entries* (Chicago, American Library Association, second edition, 1949).

Rules for descriptive cataloging in the Library of Congress (Washington, Government Printing Office 1949).

These two codes conjointly took the place of the AA *Code* in US cataloguing practice. In the period preceding acceptance and in the period following, cataloguers continued to evince much discontent with the complexity and lack of principles in codification of rules.

Between 1936 and 1939 both Library Associations co-operated in preparation for a new joint code but the outbreak of war put an end to British participation. The ALA proceeded independently and produced their 'preliminary' second edition of the *Code* in 1941 in two parts 1 'entry and heading', 2 'description of book', in which the 174 rules of the AA *Code* had grown to 375. The 1941 version was widely assailed on the grounds of complexity, over-elaboration and too extensive enumeration of cases, the most famous attack being that of A D Osborn 'The crisis in cataloguing' *Library quarterly* 11 (4) October 1941 393-411, also printed in *Library assistant* 35 (4) April 1942 54-62 and 35 (5) May 1942 69-75.

The article has been reprinted in *Olding*. It is one of the classic statements in cataloguing theory and, certainly, one of the historical turning points in code development. Among other things, Osborn convincingly demolished the three schools of cataloguers which he described as the 'legalistic', 'perfectionist' and 'bibliographical' practitioners, and thus heralded the beginning of a new era in reappraisal of cataloguing codes and practices.

The ALA Division of Cataloging and Classification undertook revision of part 1 in 1946 and produced the 1949 code which is limited to author and title entries, the LC *Rules for descriptive cataloging* (1949) being accepted as a substitute for the abandoned part 2 of the 1941 version.

The ALA rules number 158, but with numerous sections and subsections to each rule, they occupy some 226 pages compared to the 61 pages of the AA *Code* rules. They are organised into four groups: 1 rules of entry and heading (35 rules, 81 pages); 2 personal authors: form of entry (35 rules, 42 pages); 3 corporate bodies as authors (79 rules, 91 pages); 4 geographic headings (7 rules, 5 pages). Two rules covering added entries and references complete the code. Appendices cover i) glossary ii) abbreviations in headings iii) rules of style iv) translation.

The 'introduction' states that the ALA *Rules* 'are intended to represent the best or the most general current practice in cataloging . . . the rules are not few nor are they, in total, simple . . . exceptions or qualifications are made when too strict an application of a general rule would result in a heading not giving the most direct approach ...'

While it may be said that the arrangement of the rules is better than AA, that it lists more forms of literature and that the examples of the rules are better and more plentiful, yet to many of its critics it represented the continuance of the 'legalistic' approach criticised years before by Osborn.

'The codes became a maze of legalistic bypaths . . . an infinite variety of intricate exceptions to rules and exceptions to exceptions, each set up to provide for some case of suspected convenience.' Paul S Dunkin, who made this comment, records criticisms of ALA (1949) and appraisals of the LC *Rules for descriptive cataloging* in his article 'Criticisms of current cataloging practice' *Library quarterly* 26 (4) October 1956 286-302. He points out the contrast in the two codes, 'twins by fiat of ALA', in that one (LC) looked ahead, and one (ALA) looked back. The LC *Rules* were based firmly on principles developed in a preceding study by Herman Henkle *Studies of descriptive cataloging: a report to the librarian of Congress* (1946), principles that called for a consideration of logical purpose linked with simplification and brevity (*eg* bibliographical elements in a book to follow a set order regardless of their appearance on the title page; author's name to appear only once in entry). LC *Rules for descriptive cataloging: supplement 1949-51* (Washington, 1952), carried this trend further with such statements as that description should be limited to information readily available in the work being catalogued; that each new personal name entry would now be established in the form given in the work . . . provided that it conforms to ALA entry rules and is not so similar to a previously established name as to give basis for suspicion that both names refer to the same person (the 'no conflict' policy); that the 1949 *Rules for description* should be applied only to reference works and scholarly and rare material, and that most other material should

receive 'limited cataloguing' *(eg illus* to cover all kinds of illus- ~~minor change~~
trations).

Thus while the ALA *Rules* (1949) tended to reflect a traditionalist
enumerative complexity, the LC *Rules* moved towards the increasing demands of cataloguers for more simplicity and brevity.

A D Osborn reviewed the ALA *Rules* (1949) very critically in 'ALA
rules for author and title entries' *Library journal* 74 (13) July
1949 1012-1013, but found more to praise in the LC rules in
' Review of the LC 1949 code' *Library journal* 75 (9) 1950 763-64.
J H Shera ' Review of the 1949 code' *Library quarterly* 20 (2)
April 1950 147-50 noted, inter alia, the sheer growth in bulk of
the rules. L Jolley ' Some recent developments in cataloguing in
the USA' *Journal of documentation* 6 (2) June 1950 70-82, provided an authoritative assessment of the two codes, examining
them carefully against the discussion and demands that produced
them.

More recently *Bakewell* (p 35) has maintained that the two
codes 'made strange bedfellows' and he considers the ALA *Rules* to
be pedantic and more 'likely to result in a bio-bibliographical tool
rather than an efficient location tool' (p 34). *Horner* (p 75) points
out that the LC *Rules* provided the 'raw material' for subsequent
developments.

Towards a new code

The 1949 edition of the ALA *Rules* did not produce an easy peace
amongst cataloguers in the US or elsewhere. The American Library
Association, in 1951, invited Lubetsky to prepare his critical study
of cataloguing rules and in this same year the Library Association's
Cataloguing Rules Subcommittee was re-convened for the first
time since the second world war. H A Sharp ' Current research in
cataloguing' in chapter two of *Piggott* gives an account of the re-
constitution of the Subcommittee and of the beginnings of a re-
newed collaboration of the two Associations with a view to producing a second Anglo-American joint code.

The British Subcommittee spent several not very fruitful years
in consideration of the already obsolescent 1949 *Rules.* One
development of note, however, was their decision, upon examination of those matters upon which the two Associations disagreed
in 1908, to discard the British alternatives and to agree to follow
the American rules as they appeared in the 1949 edition. Accounts

of the LA Cataloguing Rules Subcommittee's work appear in *Library Association record* 57 (9) September 1955 352-353; 58 (7) July 1956 274; 60 (3) March 1958 89; 62 (8) August 1960 248-53.

As has been noted, Lubetzky's publication in 1953 of his *Cataloging rules and principles* came out strongly against the codification of catalogue rules via the elaborate and complex enumeration of innumerable ' cases ' and pointed a way towards the possible establishment of a less complex code based upon well-defined principles recognising more generalised ' conditions '. It was widely welcomed and Lubetzky was appointed editor of the new code. In 1957 his first drafts were received by the British Committee. Later drafts indicated that comments and suggestions made by the British Committee through correspondence had been taken into account.

In 1960 Lubetzky produced his *Code of cataloging rules: author and title entry; an unfinished draft* (ALA 1960) which provided a radical new shape to the rules and in which the author wished to demonstrate a departure from ' formalism ' to ' functionalism '. CCR was, like his previous work, generally welcomed by the progressives but there was evidence of worry on the part of those whom L Jolley has called the ' neo-conservatives ', about such things as the probable costs of the extensive changes that would have to be effected in the catalogues if such rules were adopted.

One British librarian who has played a key role in rules revision is A H Chaplin of the British Museum, both by his participation in US cataloguing conferences (*eg* see his article 'A universal cataloguing code' *Library quarterly* 26 (4) October 1956 87-89) and in his function as organizing secretary of the International Conference on Cataloguing Principles held in Paris in 1961.

A draft statement of cataloguing principles based upon Lubetzky's *Code of cataloging rules* was submitted to the conference for discussion along with working papers on the various problems of rules prepared by various delegates. A final version of the ' Statement of principles ' was adopted and participants agreed to work in their various countries for revised rules which would be in agreement with the accepted principles.

Chaplin gives an interesting account of the events leading up to this conference, which resulted from a working group set up by IFLA in 1954 in ' International Conference on Cataloguing Principles 1: organization ' *Journal of documentation* 19 (2) June 1963

41-45; while in the following article in the same issue L Jolley
' International Conference on Cataloguing Principles 2: thoughts
after Paris ', pages 47-62, provides a useful assessment of the conference with intelligent comment on the working papers. (He
notes, wryly, that the statement of principles frequently manages
to ignore the penetrating insights of some of these papers). Among
points made by Jolley are that the statement of principles adopted
is essentially the broad draft of an outline code; that it represents
an international agreement so that future cataloguing developments must now take on an international context; that very
broadly speaking it may be considered an endorsement of Lubetzky's work.

After this ICCP Conference, contact between British and American revision committees continued and increased. The Library
Association promoted two national conferences of cataloguers
in London to discuss progress on the new code. A report of the
first conference in July 1959 was published in the *Library Association record* 62 (8) August 1960 248-253. The second conference,
held in May 1964, was reported by P A Hoare ' Cataloguing code
revision: a participant's report ' *Library Association record* 67 (1)
January 1965 10-12. C Sumner Spalding, who succeeded Seymour
Lubetzky as editor of the new code in 1962, was present and stated
that there was a feeling in the US that Lubetzky's draft had
insufficient detail to be suitable for research libraries and that he
himself found it difficult to see things in the same way, and that
it was decided to start again and re-draft, with emphasis on the
Paris principles.

The US Code Revision Committee appears to have found itself
in 1962 in the rather paradoxical position of having won international endorsement for the soundness and sanity of Lubetzky's
Code of cataloging rules and acceptance of his approaches as
embodied in the Paris *Statement of principles,* while in the United
States itself, the big libraries were viewing these two documents,
in the light of possible cataloguing revision costs, with something
less than enthusiasm. It would appear that at the Miami Conference of 1962, the Library of Congress and the Association of
Research Libraries, having agreed on what they did *not* want the
new code to do, were able to set limits to the extent to which the
Code Revision Committee could apply the Paris principles, one
result of which is found in the retention of the 'Institutions'

75

entry, whereby many of these corporate bodies continued (in the us version) to be entered under place.* Lucile M Morsch 'An incubus and a hindrance' *Library resources and technical services* 11 (4) Fall 1967 409-414 reviews the relationships of the American Library Association with the Library of Congress over the years in the matter of rules revision, stating that certainly from 1949 onwards 'neither body was free to expand or modify any detail of its cataloguing rules without the specific approval of the other'. The *dominance* of the Library of Congress is evident in her statement that 'throughout the years of preparation there was a tacit understanding . . . that the new rules had to be satisfactory to the Library'. Miss Morsch sees this dominance as not only likely to continue, but to become even stronger in the future.

The British Cataloguing Rules Sub-Committees suffered from no such restrictions, except, perhaps, the obvious one that they were committed to working on what was to be a *joint* code and there is a limit (however imponderable) to the number of differences that can be accepted before two versions cease to be versions, and become separate codes. In the event, both texts (North American Text and British Text) of the new Anglo-American Cataloguing Rules were published in 1967, bringing to conclusion some sixteen years of work on the part of a large number of librarians in North America and Britain dedicated to the purpose of making library catalogues more effective and more efficient.

AACR

1967 AACR: *Anglo-American cataloging rules: North American text* (Chicago, American Library Association 1967).
Anglo-American cataloguing rules: British text (London, Library Association 1967).

While there is a strange echo of 1908 in that, once again, there *are* British and American differences,* and while disparity might even seem to be confirmed by the fact that the two texts are physically very different in appearance, the British text printed on

* The rules for entry under place have now been deleted from the us text—see p. 79.
* These differences are gradually being reduced in number due to developments such as the deletion of rules 98 and 99 from the North American text see p 79), and the amendment of AACR in order that it may conform to ISBD (see p 95). Plans are already in hand for the preparation of a complete revision of AACR, and it is hoped that this revision will be a truly joint UK/US code and an international standard.

institutes, libraries, galleries, museums etc) were entered under place, rather than directly under name. The American text, in a footnote, explained that these rules (which were essentially a continuance of the artificial 'Societies and institutes' practice of preceding codes) 'were required primarily by the economic circumstances obtaining in many American research libraries. The cost of adapting very large existing catalogs to the provisions of the general rules for corporate bodies without such exceptions was considered to be insupportable.' However, in May, 1972, rules 98 and 99 were deleted from the North American text and it now conforms with the British text in which the rule for 'Local churches' prescribes entry in accordance ' with general rules 60-64 ' and omits completely any rule for ' certain other corporate bodies ' to be entered under place.

The above matter represented perhaps the only major conflict of principle between the two texts. Some lesser differences which may be noted occur with regard to: ' Designation of function ' in heading (comp. ed. illus. etc) mandatory in the American text, optional in British text; rule 6, 'Serials', where rules in both texts specify successive entry in cases of changes of title, but a footnote indicates that Library of Congress will continue its practice of entry under latest title; rule 23, Court rules, with a somewhat more logical heading specified in the British text; rule 24, 'Annotated editions and commentaries', which is omitted from the British text on the grounds that such editions are already covered by rule 11.

Among differences in descriptive rules may be noted: British rule 136 ' statement of editor, compiler, translator etc ' which provides for such statement to precede or follow the edition statement according to whether the editor etc is associated with the work or with the edition. (There is no ' editor statement ' rule in the American text); variant specifications for insertion of reprint date (American rule 141, British rule 142); British provision for recording the number of plates (in as much as they represent leaves additional to the printed pages) immediately following the recording of the number of pages, in the statement of full pagination (British rule 143 B); punctuation and diacritics (appendix V), wherein the American text simply lists the punctuation symbols and specifies the use of each throughout the body of the entry, while the British text more usefully enumerates the different parts of the entry and specifies at each point which punctuation symbols should be used.

F Bernice Field reviewed the new rules (American text) in ' The new catalog code: the general principles and the major changes' *Library resources and technical services* 10 (4) Fall 1966 421-436. The article summarises the main features of AACR and concludes that the rules ' will make catalogs easier to understand, to explain, and to use them at present. The cataloging process will be more reasonable because the rules are based on principles that are clearly explained instead of on precedents.' Michael Gorman 'A-A 1967: the new cataloguing rules' *Library Association record* 70 (2) February 1968 27-32 reviewed the British text at some length in the light of modern theory, finding some of the weak points as well as the strong points and deciding that the ' rules on *choice* of heading . . . are usually adequate and often very useful; the rules on *form* of heading or reference are rarely less than comprehensive and brilliant both in their wording and their results '.

AACR has become widely accepted throughout the English speaking world. A survey carried out in New Zealand in 1970, for instance, revealed that 37 out of the 47 libraries supplying information used AACR.

The current international scene

The Paris principles have had 'a profound effect on cataloguing throughout the world. As *Bakewell* states (p 39), a large number of countries have produced codes reflecting them. However it would be wrong to suppose that they have been accepted in their entirety by all nations. A H Chaplin notes ('Cataloguing principles: five years after the Paris conference' UNESCO *Bulletin for libraries* 21 (3) May-June 1967 140-149) that where AACR is concerned, in the final result, correspondence between it and the Principles is very close, although . . . 'both texts differ from the Principles (and from each other) in the criteria they apply for entering a serial publication under a corporate body '. He notes also that they introduce a new category of ' multi-author works ' to be entered under editor, which category is not recognised by the Principles, which would require such works to be entered under titles.

Viswanathan, C G: *Cataloguing theory and practice* (London, Blunt 3rd ed 1965). Ch 3 'Catalogue codes, origin, growth, development'.

For current developments in relation to AACR rule revisions etc, the following periodicals should be read:

Catalogue & index: periodical of the Library Association Cataloguing and Indexing Group.

Library of Congress *Processing Department Cataloguing service bulletin.*

Additions and changes in the British text of AACR are listed in an *Amendment bulletin* (no. 1- 1970-) published irregularly by the Library Association free on request.

CHAPTER SEVEN

COMPARISONS BETWEEN THE CODES

Comparison between the rules in the various codes seems all too often to require unnecessary memorising of details that are, after all, readily available for consultation in the printed pages of these working tools of the cataloguer. For this reason certain progressive library schools have now chosen to concentrate on AACR, relegating other earlier codes to an historical context. Further, in the revised syllabus of the UK Library Association's professional examinations, the subject theme 'History and development of codes' has now replaced the theme 'Comparative study of the major cataloguing codes, including their development and revision'.

Some study of the comparative treatment of certain problems can lead, however, not only to a better understanding of the problems themselves, but also to better evaluation and insight into the solutions proposed. For this reason, and for the benefit of those library schools which still require students to make detailed comparisons of codes, there follows a brief tabulation of the main intent of the rulings of the five English language codes in respect of a representative number of problems. Much work has already been done in this field (see the readings cited on p 98) and it is not necessary or desirable to survey all of the rules in all the codes. Although rule numbers are included, it is again stressed that these should *not* be memorised, nor should rules be learned 'parrot fashion'.

Where AACR is concerned, it should be remembered that a classificatory pattern has been adopted and that basic rules are, therefore, prepotent. Where form of headings for persons is concerned, for example, the basic rule for entry under 'name by which commonly identified' takes precedence, when necessary, over other more specific rules.

Heinrich refers to 'the fallacy of corporate authorship' in that provisions of official cataloguing codes assert an identity between issuing agencies and authors: 'The fallacy of corporate authorship: how its continuance prevents effective cataloguing of government documents' in American Society for Information Science, *Annual Meeting, 33rd, Philadelphia, 1970 Proceedings . . .*; vol 7 *The information conscious society;* edited by Jeanne B North, Washington, 1970, 233-235. Elizabeth Moys 'Cataloguing legislative materials: some problems' *Law librarian* 3 (1) April-July 1972 6-9 15 doubts the validity of authorship for use in headings when entering legislative works and both Elizabeth Russell 'Variations on a theme in the AACR' *Library world* 72 (847) January 1971 212-213 and Michael Gorman 'More on cataloguing' *Library world* 72 (852) June 1971 330-331 agree that AACR has made the difficulties in cataloguing conference proceedings more acute. Gorman goes so far as to suggest a return to the form heading 'Conferences'. There seems little doubt that corporate authorship will continue to be a thorn in the flesh of many cataloguers.

Elements of description in the entry

Many of the features of descriptive cataloguing have their origins in, and relate to, the practices established by the textual bibliographers. The objectives of the two disciplines are quite distinct, however, for while the textual bibliographer clinically analyses and carefully enumerates the components of the ' material object ' he has examined for the purpose of giving a comprehensive anatomical description, the cataloguer is principally concerned with providing, within the array of entries in the catalogue, a statement sufficient in description to identify a copy of a book or document, to distinguish one edition of it from another, and to show its bibliographical relation to other books and documents.

Curiously, the commonplace terms, ' entry, main entry, added entry, heading ' so frequently employed in the everyday work of cataloguers are not all that easy to use unambiguously in Anglo-American practice. Definitions of these terms might be compared in both texts of AACR where it will be found that *Entry,* in its primary usage, means the complete record of the bibliographical entity in the catalogue, but that it can also mean the heading under which the entry is made (American text) or, the aspect of cataloguing dealing with the choice of headings particularly for the main entry (British and American texts).

Main entry as ' the complete record of a bibliographical entity provided in a form by which the entry is to be uniformly identified and cited ' is similarly defined in both texts, but the American practice of using the terms ' entry ' and ' heading ' somewhat interchangeably is reflected in a secondary meaning added to their definition.

In the present era, when unit entry is widely employed in catalogues *ie* when the same basic descriptive details are reproduced at various points in the catalogue under whatever headings the cataloguer selects, the utility of the concept of a ' main entry ' has been questioned. More precisely, perhaps, it would be better to say the utility of the concept of ' main heading ' has been questioned. In his paper on the *British national bibliography* at the Brasenose conference, A J Wells indicated that BNB intended to experiment with ' a form of entry that does not have a main entry heading.' He added, however, that since BNB is also used as a cataloguing guide, some way would have to be found of providing main entry heading information for those who consult the BNB for this purpose. A E Jeffreys 'Alternative headings' *Catalogue and index* '(8) October 1967 4-5 also questions the validity of main entry in multi-access catalogues, suggesting that the unit card carrying full description, but without a built-in main heading, would permit more flexible arrangements of entries under any or all selected headings. He suggests that if a main heading is needed for any purpose that this could be done by adopting the convention of a tracing note which would list the main heading first on the list of tracings in every entry. The alternative headings method has been used, apparently with some success, at the University of Liverpool.

S Spalding 'Main entry: principles and counter-principles' *Library resources and technical services* 11 (4) Fall 1967 389-396 in a searching analysis of what he terms the *four* principles (title, author, category, associated name) which may at one time or another be used in the selection of main heading in both AACR and the Paris principles (both of which are framed on the concept of main entry), notes ' The need for any entry to be chosen as a *main* entry depends on the fact that there are many situations in which that entry will be the *only* approach to the work . . . we types of illustration. If the cataloguer considers particular types important they may be designated in *alphabetical* order from a given list of terms, although ' illus ' if included, will precede this designation. (3) Height in centimetres to nearest centimetre. The logic of supplying an accurate physical account of the book by stating the number of plates ' which do not form part of the sequence of pages ' is indisputable. Whether the catalogue user will readily appreciate the nice distinction between what may appear to be a numbered statement of one type of illustration located along with the pages, while other types are arranged in alphabetical order in a separate sequence is perhaps debatable.

AACR 144: *Series statement.* In revising the rules, consideration was given to the possibility of placing this element, more logically, in the body of the entry, before the collation statement. This has not taken place, but some modest success might be claimed by the British Sub-Committee in as much as the American text also accepted the more logical designation ' Series statement ' rather than ' Series note ', and gave the rule separate status, in contrast to the earlier practice of simply including it in the section on notes.

AACR 145: *Notes.* The basic purpose of this section of the entry is to provide additional information *necessary* to the description, which cannot be provided in the body of the entry. AACR specifies clearly the ' purpose, forms, content and order ' of such notes (the last section beginning with title notes and working logically through notes on various parts of the entry). Although some cataloguers have argued that bibliographies, if recorded at all, should be entered in the more formal part of the description, they are still to be listed under the contents note (145 C 9). It may be said, however, that this does give the opportunity to record, in pages, the *extent* of a valuable bibliography.

The AACR rules for monograph description (Chapter 6) are in fact in process of revision (due for publication 1974) because of an important recent development—the publication of an *International Standard Bibliographic Description.*

International Standard Bibliographic Description

For the international exchange of bibliographic information, whether in written or machine readable form, it is obviously necessary to have a generally accepted *standard* which lists: i) the *elements* to be included in the descriptive part of an entry; ii) the *order* in which the elements are to be cited; and iii) the *punctuation* which is to be used to separate the elements. An International Working Party was set up by the International Meeting of Cataloguing Experts in Copenhagen in 1969 to study the possibilities for an International Standard Bibliographic Description (ISBD) for monographs. Such a standard was subsequently drawn up and was officially adopted by the IFLA Committee on Cataloguing at its meeting in Liverpool in 1971 (*International Standard Bibliographic Description* London, IFLA Committee on Cataloguing 1971).* Chapter 6 of AACR is being amended in order to conform to the new standard and the BNB is already making use of it.

ISBD divides the elements of the description into seven areas: 1) Title and statement of authorship; 2) Edition; 3) Imprint; 4) Collation; 5) Series; 6) Notes; 7) ISBN, binding and price. Overall ISBD does not differ appreciably from AACR. The two major changes are the inclusion of an *obligatory* author statement following the title information and the introduction of a system of standard punctuation. The latter permits quick identification of the elements even by a user who is totally unfamiliar with the language of the description. Each area, *eg* imprint area, collation area, etc, is separated from the next by point-space-dash-space (. —) unless separation is clearly indicated by paragraphing or typography. The author statement is separated from the title by a diagonal slash (/).

The following sample entries enable a comparison to be made between descriptive cataloguing by 1) AACR, 1967 and 2) ISBD:

> **Pratley, Gerald**
> The cinema of Otto Preminger, by Gerald Pratley. London: Zwemmer, 1971.
> 192p.; illus., ports. 16cm. (The international film guide series)

1 Entry by AACR (British text).
The author statement may be omitted when the author's name is

permanently associated with the catalogue entry whatever its function, *ie* when a main author entry is used in full as a unit entry.

> **Pratley, Gerald**
> The cinema of Otto Preminger / by Gerald Pratley.— London: Zwemmer, 1971.
> 192p.: ill., ports.; 16cm.— (The international film guide series)
> ISBN 0 302 02152 3   Pbk.: £0.90

2 Entry by ISBD.
The author statement is obligatory.

Issue number 105 of the Library of Congress Cataloguing Service *Bulletin* November 1972 was devoted primarily to ISBD and to its effect on AACR and Library of Congress cataloguing data. It is expected that LC will implement the rules of the International Standard Bibliographic Description during 1974.

The above information could more accurately be said to refer to ISBD(M), the 'M' indicating 'monographs'. A further standard bibliographic description, which will be published in March 1974, is now in existence. This is ISBD(S), the 's' indicating 'serials'. Lawrence G Livingston writes about 'International Standard Bibliographic Description for serials' in *Library resources and technical services* 17 (3) Summer 1973 293-298.

No code of cataloguing rules need be adopted in its entirety by a particular library and certain elements of the description may, of course, be omitted if desired. In fact, the tendency in descriptive cataloguing has generally been towards simplicity and brevity and away from rather pedantic pseudo-bibliographical style that 'full' cataloguing was often alleged to require. However, there is nothing new in this—Cutter's descriptive rules 223-297 recognised the requirements of 'short, medium and full' cataloguing and his frequent comments 'short will omit . . .' or 'I do not see why even full should use this . . .' are evidence of his thoughts in this direction, although these provisions for differential treatment were hardly conducive to the uniformity or practice nowadays sought. Mary Piggott 'Uniformity in descriptive cataloguing' *Libri* 13 (1) 1963

45-54 investigates the elements of description in different kinds of catalogues and national bibliographies, her article being written in the light of the agreements on choice and forms of heading at Paris in 1961.

Currently, many library automation programmes, such as those at Bath University Library and Loughborough University of Technology, cater for minimal cataloguing input with maximum flexibility of output.

READINGS

Many of the readings cited in the previous chapter are also relevant here. Additional material includes:

Bakewell Ch 4 'Some special problems of the author/title catalogue'.

Hanson, J C M: *A comparative study of cataloguing rules, based on the Anglo-American code of 1908* (Chicago University Press 1939). Surveys, on the framework of AA Code, nineteen codes of rules including the BM rules (1927 edition), Cutter and Vatican code (first edition 1931).

Jolley Ch 2 'The author catalogue' provides a penetrating commentary on ALA, AA and BM rulings for entry. Chapter 3 'Corporate authorship', gives a comprehensive exposition of this problem.

Lewis, P R: 'Points of departure: a first comparison of the 1908 and 1967 codes' *Catalogue & index* (9) Jan 1968 10-15.

Ranganathan, S R: *Headings and canons: comparative study of five catalogue codes* (Madras, Vizwanathan; London, Blunt 1955). Compares Cutter, Prussian instructions, Vatican, ALA (1949) and Ranganathan's own Classified catalogue code.

Sharp Ch 23 and 24 'Comparative study of cataloguing codes'. Compares BM, Cutter and AA.

CHAPTER EIGHT

SPECIAL PROBLEMS OF CERTAIN CATEGORIES OF LIBRARY MATERIALS

Libraries have for long included in their stock material other than printed books—manuscripts, maps and pictorial material being obvious examples. Newer forms of ' storable ' records such as films and sound recordings, and variant forms of presentation of print such as microfilm, have emerged and proliferated in recent times, and many libraries have found it increasingly necessary to their purposes to widen their scope and become resource centres administering information presented in a variety of physical forms. Consequently, cataloguing practice has been extended necessarily to include the listing and indexing of this material and to deal with the problems encountered.

Because these materials are, in essence, similar to printed books in that they are records with intellectual content, there can be no fundamental difference in the application of general cataloguing principles to them. Differences centre more particularly on their variation in physical form. There are, however, three basic problems:

1 Since a large proportion of these materials do not have authors in the conventional sense, what element should be chosen as the main entry heading? 'Author equivalent' is a most variable and sometimes an elusive factor. There is the fairly obvious choice of composer for music scores but who is primarily responsible, for example, for the existence of a film?

2 Since their physical form or mode of presentation is frequently quite different from that of the book, which descriptive details are required in the body of the entry and how best can they be arranged and cited? The elements of the description, particularly the collation details, vary most widely in non-book materials and it is in this area, principally, that the cataloguer

must develop special applications of general cataloguing practice.

3 Should the catalogue entries for these variant materials be included in the general book catalogue(s) of the library to form multi-media catalogues, or should they be provided for in separate catalogues, indexes and lists? It is interesting to note that US practice has tended towards inclusion of special materials in the general catalogues, whilst European library practice has tended more towards the provision of the separate catalogues, lists or indexes.

This question of the desirability of separate catalogues and indexes is one of the recurring themes in an article by Jay E Daily ' The selection, processing, and storage of non-print materials: a critique of the *Anglo-American cataloguing rules* as they relate to the newer media' *Library trends* October 1967 283-289. The writer concedes that the rules in Part III of AACR when 'viewed retrospectively as a summary . . . are superior' but, in the course of the article, as he comments in turn on the rules for films, gramophone records and pictures, he criticises what might be described as the underlying philosophy of trying to tie the rules for such materials too tightly to the pattern established for books. He argues strongly for the treatment of 'each collection of non-book material as a separate and special entity, the use of which is inevitably governed by the nature of the material itself' and urges the use of book catalogues, edge-notched card systems or co-ordinate indexes using multiple entries as the occasion may demand.

A recent report by Tony Trebble (*op cit*) tends to reinforce Daily's arguments. Trebble suggests that 'a multi-media collection is not a unified concept but in fact remains several collections each of different media. Most users in most libraries seek materials in terms of form rather than subject, so that the integration of both stocks and catalogues should be positively resisted'.

The years since the publication of AACR have witnessed a vastly increased interest in 'non-book' (a most unsatisfactory term) materials and, in the light of rapid developments in the media industry,* two attempts have been made to produce draft revisions of the relevant section (part III) of these rules. In Canada, a completely rewritten and updated version of a preliminary work which was first issued in 1970 has recently been published: *Nonbook*

---

* A speaker at a London seminar in October, 1973, reminded his audience that when AACR was formulated cartridges were confined to the world of firearms!

materials; the organisation of integrated collections, by Jean Riddle Weihs, Shirley Lewis and Janet Macdonald, in consultation with the CLA/ALA/AECT/EMAC/CAML Advisory Committee on the Cataloguing of Nonbook Materials (Ottawa, Canadian Library Association 1973). In the UK, collaboration between the National Council for Educational Technology (now the Council for Educational Technology of the United Kingdom) and the Library Association has resulted in *Non-book materials cataloguing rules: integrated code of practice and draft revision of the Anglo-American rules British text Part III,* prepared by the Library Association Media Cataloguing Rules Committee (London, National Council for Educational Technology with the Library Association 1973). Despite Daily's plea, both of these sets of rules are basically compatible with those for books and printed materials. However, the British work, already affectionately known as 'Lancet' (LA/NCET), was designed first and foremost as a self-contained code of practice in its own right and the compilers consider that a satisfactory relationship with AACR would best follow from—rather than precede —the attainment of this primary objective:

'In the non-book materials for which these rules are intended the creative responsibility for intellectual or artistic content is characteristically shared among several persons or bodies, performing between them a variety of functions, the relative importance of which to the work is difficult to determine, and which often permit no analogy with the authors of books and texts. These materials are therefore regarded as constituting an exception to the General Principles determining the entry of books and book-like materials...'

Priority is therefore given firstly to the establishment for each item of a body of descriptive information, and secondly to the anticipation of the most effective points of access to this information, for use as headings in the catalogue. This method is akin to the alternative headings approach to cataloguing (see p 92), although these rules do cater for the addition to the 'standard item description' of a 'primary name heading', which becomes a permanent element of the standard catalogue entry.

Important omissions from the British draft are manuscripts, maps and music. The Media Cataloguing Rules Committee recommend that rules relating to these materials should be taken out of the present part III of AACR and regrouped in closer relationship with parts I and II, as they have a closer affinity with written and printed records than those materials for which rules are provided, namely motion pictures and filmstrips, sound recordings and pictures, designs, etc. A further omission is the provision of rules for the cataloguing of computer records, a regretful decision made because time did not permit of sufficient consideration being given to this particular category before publication.

Cataloguing rules for machine readable files *are* included in the Canadian code and this work also includes suggestions for the *storage* of various media. As in the British rules, manuscripts and printed music have been omitted but maps are included. The Canadian rules are most definitely structured so that all materials, both book and non-book, can be integrated into a single, unified list of holdings and the general rules call for a main entry under author, where one can be identified, otherwise entry is under title. Although originating in Canada, these rules are accepted by the American Library Association and this body was represented on the consultant Advisory Committee. The Australian School Library Association has also endorsed the work.

The Canadian rules are reasonably simple, general rules being followed by additions and exceptions for each individual medium, *eg* audiorecords, dioramas, models, slides, etc, arranged alphabetically. There are many clear examples and a useful index is appended. The British rules also contain preliminary general rules in chapter one, but this is then followed not by individual media but by three general 'categories', *ie* chapter two deals with graphics and three-dimensional representations; chapter three with motion pictures; and chapter four with sound recordings. An index to specific materials included in each of these categories is provided. The British arrangement tends to be more complex and not as easy to use as the Canadian, but, on the other hand, the British rules are less 'author conscious', more analytical in their approach, and are, therefore, perhaps more suited to their purpose.

During the preparation of the British and Canadian rules, information and ideas were exchanged, and the British Committee was represented at meetings of the AACR author bodies (with AECT observers) in Dallas, June 1971, and Chicago, June 1972. At the latter of these, preliminary drafts of the British general rules were examined in some detail and, so the introduction to the British code informs us, 'recommended in principle as a basis for the revision of AACR'.* However, it is perhaps questionable whether either of these sets of rules should be used for AACR revision. If the Librarian of the University of Bradford is right in that 'We must stop thinking of books, films and sound recordings as completely different things' (University of Bradford *Annual report of the librarian, session 1971-2* quoted by Norman Roberts 'University Libraries' *Library Association record* 75 (11) November 1973 219-221), then would it not be better to completely restructure AACR into *two* parts only, 'Heading' and 'Description' (in either order) with generally applicable rules, amplified and clarified as necessary for problems specific to particular media?

The British and Canadian rules are not the only recent attempts to come to grips with the difficult problems associated with the cataloguing of various media. A third edition of the AECT standards was issued in 1972 (Association for Educational Communications and Technology *Information Science Committee Standards for cataloguing non-print material* 3rd ed Washington, AECT 1972) and in the same year Anthony Croghan carried on 'his fight to assert the right of the individual to frame codes' (*A code of rules for, with an exposition of, integrated cataloguing of non-book media* London, Coburgh Publications 1972).

Films

Problems: A basic problem exists in that reels and canisters of film cannot be scanned or handled in the same way as most other forms of record; consequently examination, even by the cataloguer for the purposes of cataloguing, must be kept to a minimum. This difficulty of physical accessibility to the record further imposes on the cataloguer the necessity of providing as far as possible all descriptive detail likely to be required by users, up to and including a summary or synopsis of content of the film record.

Main entry heading: Any film can be the result of the conjoint work of many diverse contributors, so films are most commonly identified by title, which is consequently the recognised element

* Late in 1973, the LC stated (Library of Congress *Processing Department Cataloguing service bulletin* (107) December 1973 2) that work was to proceed on a draft revision of ch 12 of AACR 'Motion pictures and filmstrips' and that the draft would be based on three major publications: LA/NCET, the Canadian rules and *Standards for cataloguing non-print media* (*op cit* this page). Another document, *Nonprint media guidelines* produced by an 'ad hoc' task force under the chairmanship of Pearce S Grove, will also be taken into consideration.

for the heading of the main entry. It should be noted, however, that a problem exists here in that titles can vary widely (or entirely differ) upon release of film in different countries (and so can the language in the sound track).

Cataloguing rules vary in their approach to this problem. The UNESCO film catalogue rules, for instance, prescribe entry under title of language version in hand, while the ASLIB code (1963) recommends the establishment of a heading under the title of release in country of origin. The LA/NCET rules note that a uniform title may be required to bring together the variously titled copies.

Description: Following upon citation of title, LA/NCET specifies the following elements of description: place of publication or production and name of production company; sponsor or advertiser; date of publication or release and of first transmission as appropriate; place of distribution and distributor; physical form designator (*eg* cinefilm, EVR, videotape) and technical specification (*eg* packaging, such as cassette, gauge of film, projecting speed, etc); series; and notes (including a summary describing concisely and objectively the content of the film and other information such as additional credits, *eg* the cast, related material, copyright details, etc).

Subject cataloguing: No essential divergence from conventional practice. The *British national film catalogue* (Lōndon, BNFC Ltd 1963-) should be examined as an example of the classified form using UDC classification. The *Library of Congress catalog: motion pictures and filmstrips* (Washington, Library of Congress, 1953-) has an alphabetical main entry section complemented by an alphabetical subject index based on LC subject headings. Both catalogues are bi-monthlies with cumulations. The indexing by producers, distributors, commentators, etc in BNFC should be noted. The headings in the LC catalogue are qualified by the descriptive phrases ' motion picture ' or ' filmstrip ' since they are based on printed card entries available for insertion in general catalogues.

BNFC should not be confused with BUFC, which is the way in which the extremely useful British Universities Film Council catalogue is referred to. Designed to alleviate the problem of finding and selecting films and other audio visual material, it was first published in 1960 and again in 1968 under the title *Films for universities* but the latest 1973 issue is entitled *Audio-visual materials for higher education.*

Horner *Special . . . (op cit* ch 3) deals comprehensively with the cataloguing of films. D Grenfell is also worth reading on this subject. He contributed Chapter 12 of J Burkett and T S Morgan (*op cit*) and his two articles 'Cataloguing of films' *Librarian* 47 (4) April-May 1958 62-64 and 'Standardization in film cataloguing' *Journal of documentation* 15 (2) June 1959 81-92 discuss the codification of film cataloguing practice, in which, it should be noted, there is no scarcity of codes, since Library of Congress rules (1958), UNESCO rules (1956), National Film Archive rules (1960) and ASLIB rules (1963) have all been formulated, with the above being joined by AACR (1967). Chapter 12, rules 220-229—replacing the Library of Congress rules—and AACR is, as noted, in process of revision.

Music scores

Problems: Musical notation is a truly international medium, and works by the major composers have long been published in many countries by many publishers with title pages in many languages. Many works have titles based upon their form, and popular titles as well (*eg* Beethoven's Sonata in C sharp minor, opus 27 number 2, is also popularly known as the ' Moonlight sonata '). Again, music publishers in every country have displayed a remarkable lack of uniformity in such matters as translation of the title or even the citation of the elements of it in any kind of standard order. Such matters have created for the music cataloguer a condition whereby the title page of the music score is not necessarily as sacrosanct as in other printed documents and, in fact, sometimes he may have to use it merely as a basis, deriving additional needed information from standard works of musicology.

AACR 233 recommends the establishment of uniform titles so that all variously titled editions and arrangements of a work may be collocated. The selection of the language for a uniform title can create a problem also, for whatever decision may be taken on the use of a particular language, there will be some works equally known and some perhaps better known by title in another language. AACR 234 recommends that ' the uniform title is established in the language of the original title, unless a translated title (in English or otherwise) is better known ' a rule that inevitably must put the burden of decision of ' better known ' form on the cataloguer.

Description: There is no essential disagreement among codes upon choice of composer as heading for main entry. It might be noted that AACR 19 B 'Librettos' provides an interesting case study in the Anglo-American cataloguing rules. Rule AACR 19 for 'Other related works' provides for entry of many related works (one and a half pages of examples) under their own author and title. AACR 19 B for 'Librettos' is cited as an *optional* exception to this rule and permits entry under composer. A further subsection to AACR 19 B provides that if 'published as a literary work or without reference to a particular music setting, enter it under its author'. An example of open-ended provision, and also perhaps that the era of 'exceptions to exceptions' is not yet ended.

TITLE: which may be the name of an opera or vocal work, or in the case of other musical works, may be composed of the following elements: form (*eg* sonata, trio, concerto, mass etc); form number (if any—sonata no 2, concerto no 8, etc); instrumentation or voices ('for violin, viola and 'cello', 'for soprano and alto'); key ('in B flat'); opus number (this accepted musical convention for precise identification, though widely regarded as immutable, can be found to vary between one publisher's edition and another).

IMPRINT: The *publisher* is frequently important to the musician for identification of a particular edition wanted. The *date* is a relatively unimportant factor in scores and often enough is absent from the publication. AACR 245 D recommends, in the absence of a printed date, that a plate number or publisher's number should be added after the *supplied* imprint date.

COLLATION: *Number of pages, height* (in cms). AACR 246 B provides for the recording of parts, or score and parts in this section, noting that works issued in score only, should have the statement of the score included in the title transcript.

NOTES: Will be frequently used to elucidate the many features that can be present and may not be recorded in title *eg arrangements* ('orchestral work arranged for two pianos'); *language(s)* of works or libretto; *contents* of collections of pieces.

Subject cataloguing: Subject cataloguing of scores demonstrates the dominance of musical form, whereby entries are grouped under quartets, symphonies, concertos etc, frequently subdivided by instrumentation. The *Library of Congress catalog*: *music and phonorecords* (Washington, Library of Congress 1953-) provides good examples of subject headings in its separate subject index, while the *British catalogue of music* (London, BNB 1957-) bases its subject entries on a specially developed faceted classification scheme.

Horner *Special . . . (op cit)* deals with the cataloguing of music and describes at some length (p 111-135) that wide-ranging survey of the problems of music cataloguing, the International Association of Music Libraries *Code international de catalogage de la musique* (Frankfurt, London, Peters, 1957- 3v out of 5 so far been published) which has text in German, English and French. Volume one of this code 'The author catalogue', surveys the comparative practice of a group of large libraries from many countries, and provides vivid illustrations of music cataloguing complexities in the form of twelve facsimile title pages, each exemplifying certain problems and accompanied by comparisons of the entries for these works in the various library catalogues. Volume two takes the form of a 'limited' code and appears to be intended to be used alone. Volume three contains rules for full cataloguing.

Relevant sections of general works on music librarianship, *eg* E T Bryant *Music librarianship: a practical guide* (London, Clarke 1959); Lionel Roy McColvin and Harold Reeves *Music libraries ...*; completely rewritten, revised and extended by Jack Dove (London, Deutsch 1965); and Brian Redfern *Organising music in libraries* (London, Bingley: Hamden, Conn, Linnet 1966), are also valuable.

Music recordings

Problems: Obviously a repetition of those for music scores further complicated by the physical form of the sound record. The label and the sleeve provide the equivalents of the title page. (It should be noted that the sleeve often contains programme notes, lists of soloists, synopsis and much other needed information.)

Description: In addition to the details required for the citation of the music, elements of the gramophone record entry should include: imprint (name of *record company, manufacturer's catalogue number*); collation (*sides*—double or single, *size ie* diameter in inches, *speed ie* 33⅓ rpm 45 rpm etc, *kind of recording ie* microgroove, stereophonic); performance (orchestra, conductor, soloist, vocalist etc.); notes (contents of collections).

Classification of the records is widely considered unnecessary in most collections, since users normally do not approach the shelves or containers for browsing as they can do with books. Accession number order, or even grouping by manufacturer's catalogue numbers can suffice on the shelves, and the catalogue must provide the mechanism for retrieval by 1 *composer* 2 *title* (note that a high proportion of records will have main entry under title since they can frequently focus on the nature of the music *eg* ' Folk music of Kashmir ' or performer ' di Stefano sings Neapolitan songs ') 3 *performer*. Added entries for soloists, conductors or orchestras should be made.

Since many records carry different works on each side, and can often contain many different items, analytical entries are frequently required.

Horner *Special* . . . (*op cit*) also deals with the cataloguing of music recordings and S A Somerville 'Cataloguing of gramophone records' *Librarian* 48 (5) July 1959 97-99 discusses record problems and gives examples of practice. Procedures in some American libraries are summarised by Mary Jane Sunder in 'Organisation of recorded sound' *Library resources and technical services* 13 (1) Winter 1969 93-98. The *Library of Congress catalog: music and phonorecords* (cited above) provides good examples of main entries and subject headings for gramophone records.

C Barnes ' Classification and cataloguing of spoken records in academic libraries ' *College and research libraries* 28 (1) January 1967 49-52 describes some classification schemes for this type of recorded material, and argues for the generous use of added entries in the catalogue. With regard to the question of entries being integrated in the general library catalogue or being filed in a separate catalogue, he states that the ideal solution is to do both.

Maps

Problems: Maps have no title page in the conventional sense. AACR 212 B recommends that, while the title may be taken from any part of the face of the map, preference over a marginal title should be given to a title within the border of a map, or within a cartouche (the ornamental scroll with inscription often found on older maps).

AACR 210 and 212 in recommending main entry heading under person or corporate body responsible for the informational content (*eg* cartographer, publisher etc) seek a logical equivalent of book author in this way, but, except in the case of specialists seeking rare and antique maps, this is not a very common or probable

on computer-produced map catalogue' *Australian library journal* 21 (6) July 1972 245-252. 'The Library of Congress: computerised map cataloguing project' is the title of an article by Walter W Ristow and David K Carrington *International library review* 2 (3) July 1970 391-397.

Microforms

Problems: The most fundamental problem is by no means confined to the cataloguing of the microform, but affects such aspects as storage, organisation and use. It is the variation in the *types* of microforms between transparent and opaque forms of different shapes and sizes. (*Microfilms*, in reels of different lengths with widths of 16mm, 35mm, 70mm; *microfiche*, transparent sheet film of various dimensions usually needing protective envelopes; *micro-opaque cards*, again of various dimensions, 5 × 3, 9 × 6 inches, which may carry images on one or on both sides.) The construction of an entry for a microform will naturally follow the cataloguing practice related to the original book or document of which it is a variant copy.

Description of the microform may be entered *below the entry for the original*, which will have been entered according to the general rules.

Description: Includes such elements as a medium designation (microfilm, microfiche, micro-opaque); an imprint; and a physical description, *eg* number of pieces (reels, sheets, cards, boxes), and size of film or mount.

Subject cataloguing: There need be no essential difference in the subject cataloguing of microforms from those principles applied to books, and entries can be inserted in the general catalogue with the notes and details of the microform, drawing attention to their different physical form. But the question of how far analytical cataloguing should proceed in the case of microform publications containing voluminous works poses a fair problem. D T Richnell 'Microtexts: acquisition and organization' chapter 14 of J Burkett and T S Morgan (*op cit*) p 152-165, states this problem clearly, instancing a microprint publication containing more than 5,000 plays whereby, if each title were to be analytically catalogued, the library would have a major cataloguing problem on its hands. He concludes that libraries, in general, should avoid making the attempt to provide separate entries for items in *general* collections but rather should provide maximum publicity for the presence of such collections in the library. D Brockway 'A new look at the cataloguing of microfilm' *Library resources* 4 (4) Fall 1960 323-330, puts forward the view that too much descriptive detail concerning the original document tends to be inserted on the entry for the microfilm and such description should be limited.

Incunabula

Incunabula (books printed before 1501) provide the cataloguer with the problem of producing entries based upon the practices of descriptive bibliography. Detailed analysis and recording of the features, physical and textual, of the particular copy is considered desirable for the purposes of possible comparison with other extant copies, and description should result in the careful transcription of the title page or colophon recording every detail exactly, down to the presence of printer's ornaments. The imprint will record *place of printing, printer's name* and *date of printing*. The collation should contain statements of *format; signatures; number of leaves* or *foliation; number of columns* per page; *number of lines* on page or column; *type area* in mms; *type style*. The presence of *capitals, catchwords, illustrations, printer's devices* must be indicated. The bibliographical note will cover description of the binding, peculiarities and imperfections of the copy catalogued, and references to the work in standard bibliographies of incunabula.

In view of the existence of such standard bibliographies, containing detailed descriptions of nearly all of the existing incunabula, AACR chapter 8 'Incunabula' formulates its rules on the basis that in a general catalogue only a short-title form of entry in conventional style will be required, the collation statement therein being followed by bibliographical reference (AACR 184), to a printed description in one or more of the published authoritative catalogues. The work by F R Goff *Incunabula in American libraries: a third census of fifteenth century books* (New York, Bibliographical Society of America, 1964) is particularly cited for this purpose. However AACR 185 (notes) does provide for such items as signatures and foliation to be specified, if they are not given in a cited source.

In 'A computer-based census and local handlist system for incunabula' (*Computers and the humanities* 6 (2) November 1971

95-102) Jessica Harris, Theodore Hines and Ralph Scott describe a computer-based catalogue for the 850 incunabula owned by Columbia University and it is suggested that this could serve as a model for other collections and as a contribution to an eventual national census.

Manuscripts

Manuscripts in a library may range from items such as literary mss, bound collections of an individual's letters, diaries etc having an author and a title page and to which 'conventional principles' can be applied, to miscellaneous documents and loose sheets such as wills, deeds, receipts etc, for which the cataloguer must supply a title and a summary of content sufficient for description. The 'book form' manuscripts can be dealt with generally in accordance with the rules for printed books so long as the entry clearly records in a note that the item catalogued is an original mss. The other forms of mss tend to force the catalogue to return to its historical origins and become more or less an inventory. A serial identity number may be supplied to each item and this may be used as the simplest basis of arrangement of the main entries, or, depending upon the nature of the collection, arrangement may be made under place or under date. In any case, special indexes covering names of persons, places, events will have to be provided to supplement the main entry sequence. The catalogue of such mss necessarily becomes a separate catalogue and is not usually compatible with the general library catalogue.

However, in chapter 10 'Manuscripts' of the AACR, emphasis is necessarily on compatibility with the general rules for printed materials (even if it may often result in the establishment of a heading by provision of what is merely an associated name). Rules 201 to 204 provide very well for the literary forms (medieval and modern); letters, speeches and lectures; legal papers; on the same principles of author and title entry developed in the general rules. (The principal examples for anonymous mss are to be found in the general rule 103, 'Works of unknown authorship without title'.) The form of the manuscript (holograph, ms, typescript etc) is to be shown in the first paragraphed note. Rules 205 to 207 provide for entry and description of collections of mss, establishing a preference order for main heading of 1 person or corporate body upon which collection is centred, 2 collector's name,

3 name of collection (if any), 4 title supplied by cataloguer. Michael Jasenas 'Cataloging small manuscript collections' *Library resources and technical services* 7 (3) Summer 1963, 264-273 describes a scheme used at Cornell University whereby the cataloguing entry is focused upon the assembly of a 'cataloguable unit', consisting of gatherings of mutually related mss items.

Illustrations, prints, slides

Cataloguing codes such as AACR are concerned only with author and title and generally with the integration of entries for all types of material in a general library catalogue. In the case of illustrations, however, detailed descriptive cataloguing would seem superfluous as few illustration collections are limited merely to forms with such easily ascertainable details. More often, the picture collection will contain an extensive mixture of all kinds of pictorial material including photographs, illustrations clipped from periodicals, brochures (and even books), post-cards etc. In such collections, descriptive details in the entry as a means of approach to an illustration tend to be of limited value, and the main problem centres on the subject cataloguing method and subject arrangement of the material. In fairness to AACR, it must be said that the introductory notes to the chapter recognise this fact—'most pictorial works in libraries may be economically and efficiently serviced by arrangement in files by subject or other category . . . in accordance with the needs, size, and specialisation of a particular library, some of the descriptive details may be either simplified or elaborated and the number of added entries increased or decreased'.

The Canadian revision of AACR also recognises that 'not all library materials warrant the expenditure involved in complete cataloguing and processing'. It is recommended that 'ephemeral' materials should be arranged alphabetically by subject or systematically, appropriate guide cards being inserted in the catalogue proper.

C H Gibbs-Smith 'Visual materials' chapter eleven, p 117-126, of Burkett and Morgan (*op cit*) describes the system used in the Hulton Library based on four subject groups (portraits, topographical, historical, modern) and questions the need for 'card indexes', on the presumption that the scheme should be self-indexing. D Mason's 'Illustrations' chapter two of his *Primer* (*op cit*) mentions a comparable broad scheme used in the New York Public Library (views, personalities, general) but also instances collections classified by DC with subject indexes.

D Rogers ' Works of art ' *Catalogue and index* (5) Jan 1967 4-6, and, (6) April 1967 10-11 deals in depth with the requirements of cataloguing original works of art, finding it necessary to specify more descriptive elements than are provided for in AACR.

A useful article on the rather difficult problem of cataloguing slides is Peter Havard-Williams and Stella A Watson ' The slide collection at Liverpool School of Architecture ' *Journal of documentation* 16 (1) March 1960 11-14, which describes how, with the slides arranged in accession order, cataloguing rules were formulated with the necessary emphasis on the subject catalogue and subject headings. A scheme of descriptive details used is given, but it is stated that, in practice, it was found that elaborate descriptions were unnecessary. B W Kuvshinoff 'A graphic graphics card catalog and computer index ' *American documentation* 18 (1) Jan 1967 3-9 describes a card catalogue for slides and photos in which the cards carry miniature reproductions of the pictorial material, visible data entered by typewriter, and coded data keypunched. The cards can thus be manually searched, and employed for various other manual applications, while a computer can be used to prepare indexes from the punched data.

A computer index to a university library slide collection is described in 'The computer at Santa Cruz: slide classification with automated cross-indexing' by Luraine Tansey *Picturescope* 18 (2) 1970 64-75. A classification scheme, developed for the project, facilitates browsing. 80-column punched cards give fifteen fields, the major ones being dates, country and art form. Art history predominates and style, artist or place of origin, subject matter and title are also coded.

Computer records

The Canadian rules define machine readable data files as information coded by methods that require the use of a machine (typically but not always a computer) for translation. Examples include disc packs, magnetic tape, optical character recognition, font documents and punched cards or tape.

The above definition highlights the basic problems, which are the physical form and the unintelligibility of that form. In addition such records usually lack a 'title page' equivalent and the cataloguer may be confronted with no title or many conflicting titles. Nor does the concept of 'publication' apply in the traditional sense.

If primary responsibility for the existence of a record can be attributed to some person or corporate body, this can be used as a normal author type heading. If there is no such author, entry must be under title, supplied by the cataloguer if necessary. Where there are conflicting titles, the Canadian rules recommend that the title is chosen on the basis of the author's intent, prevalence of use, or citations in reference sources.

Coded information may be transferred easily from one format to another, *eg* punched cards to magnetic tape, and the Canadian rules therefore recommend that the collation should not describe the actual physical format. Instead a statement of the 'file size' is given, *eg* 1613 logical records*, and amplified as necessary by notes. As with films, the use of a summary outlining content and explaining the collation, etc, is essential.

READINGS

Basic reading is provided by *Bakewell* (ch 7) and *Horner* (ch 20). Horner followed up his general treatise on cataloguing with a comprehensive work on *Special cataloguing* (London, Bingley 1973). The latter suffers from being published before the LA/NCET and Canadian rules could be included. The way in which the former of these codes was written is the subject of the autumn 1973 issue of *Catalogue and index* (31); Autumn 1973).

Other books on special materials include:

Burkett, J and Morgan, T S ed: *Special materials in the library* (London, LA 1963). A collection of fourteen lectures by specialists on the treatment of special materials which clearly indicate the diversity of their approaches to the various problems, including cataloguing.

Mason, Donald *A primer of non-book materials in libraries* (London, AAL 1958). Sections in each chapter deal with the cataloguing, or arrangement and indexing, of the principal special materials.

When considering the above two works, the rapid developments that have taken place in the media industry since their publication should be borne in mind.

* *Logical record* A single unit of information consisting of one or more fields or variables.

Eaton, Thelma: *Cataloguing and classification: an introductory manual* (Illinois, Illini Union Bookstore 3rd ed 1963). Ch 7 'The organisation of special materials' includes facsimile entries of LC cards based on the various LC rules for special materials. *a little aed?*

Grove, Pearce S and Clement, Evelyn G: *Bibliographic control of nonprint media* (Chicago, ALA 1972) is a useful general work.

A book which deals with a proposed computer system for the cataloguing of audio-visual materials in the UK is:

Gilbert, Leslie A and Wright, Jan W: *Non-book materials: their bibliographic control* (London, NCET 1971).

Stimulating reading is provided by:

Fothergill, Richard: *A challenge for librarians?* A report on the joint NCET/Aslib Audio Visual Group Conference on Multi-Media Resource Organisation in Higher Education, held in Hull in December 1970. (London, NCET in association with the Aslib Audio Visual Group, 1971.)

The *Impact of new media on libraries* is the subject of a report to OSTI by Tony Trebble (University of Sussex Library 1973). The author examined the practices of some 200 libraries in three continents.

In an integrated catalogue, some method of indicating the type of medium is required. Colour codes and symbols are dealt with in ch 6 'Cataloguing—communicating with the patron' of:

Hicks, Warren B and Tillin, Alma M: *Developing multi-media libraries* (London, Bowker 1970). The same chapter also deals with general cataloguing practice and Part II of this book—'The practice'—has many examples of procedures and samples of catalogue cards for various media.

The Canadian *Non-book materials: the organisation of integrated collections* (cited on p 100) does not recommend the use of either colour codes or symbols but prefers the medium designation which should be included early in the body of the entry. This work also includes some extremely useful guidelines for the care, handling and storage of various media.

CHAPTER NINE

CATALOGUING PROCESSES AND POLICIES

With the commitment of cataloguers to commonly-accepted classification schemes and cataloguing codes, and with their continual and justifiable efforts to attain standardisation in many areas of practice, it may be wondered why so much variation exists in the organisation of cataloguing operations and policies between one library and another. The answer is to be found in the simple fact that a cataloguing department and a cataloguing system, if either is to be efficient and effective, must be designed and operated to answer the specific needs of the library or library system which it serves.

The good management of cataloguing operations requires that many procedures which may be common to all cataloguing operations have to be implemented, not in a vacuum, but in exact relation to a particular library situation. Examples of these procedures are the sorting of material at the pre-cataloguing stage; the question of whether the cataloguing should be divided on a basis of function (*ie* separating or linking descriptive and subject cataloguing, or creating subject specialist cataloguers); the reproduction of cataloguing entries (or the use of printed cards); and many policies are available for adoption, such as analytical cataloguing, selective cataloguing, limited cataloguing. Obviously, the variety of library situations is very great, and is by no means limited to the differences between, say, academic and public, or special and county, but readily obtains within each group.

The professional cataloguer will develop and operate his system not solely on the basis of what he or she considers to be 'a best way' of doing this or that thing, but on the basis of careful analysis of the library system in respect of such interrelated matters as:

1 The type of library and the purpose it serves.

2 The organisation and disposition of its stock, collections, branches, departments.

3 The nature of its acquisitions.

4 The nature of the library's clientele and the number and types of catalogues which have to be provided for them.

5 The resources in staff and equipment available for cataloguing.

The notes on cataloguing processes and policies given below must be related to these considerations.

Reproduction of catalogue entries

Few technical processes in libraries have produced more invention, adaptation and improvisation than that of catalogue entry reproduction. Ever since it was realised that the same descriptive detail might well be reproduced, on card or sheaf, under a number of different headings in the catalogue, librarians have sought the ideal method of doing this. Individual systems have proliferated in libraries and have been described in library literature, each with its own claim to speed, economy, flexibility or typographical clarity. Some of the very many in general use include:

The typewriter: Still the most economical when only two or three cards are required or when, using carbon copies, a small number of sheaf entries is needed.

The *tape typewriter* produces a punched tape as well as a normal typescript image. This punched tape can be fed back into the typewriter to automatically produce further copies. Multiple copies of an entry can be obtained quickly in this way.

Wax-stencil duplicator: A wax-stencil master cut by typewriter, fastened round drum containing ink. Ink passes through cut-out stencil to copy under pressure of rotary drum. The copy is very clear, and several thousand copies are possible; reasonably economic in materials used. Disadvantages are the drying time needed for copies (and card stock must be reasonably absorbent), and the fact that no special version of duplicators (with drum-size related to smaller stencil size needed for cards) has been developed yet in the UK. Bennett, the cataloguer at Tower Hamlets Public Library, successfully uses a 'home-made' flat-bed wax stencil duplicator. He claims that this method achieves greater economy combined with greater efficiency, as compared, for instance, with the use of BNB printed cards (see also p 143/144).

Xerography: Various libraries, including the National Library of Scotland and the University of Colorado (see *Bakewell* p 210), have found the ease with which copies can be made using xerography, combined with the permanent image obtained, to be advantageous where the reproduction of cataloguing entries is concerned. In 'Break-even point for a proof-slip operation' *College research libraries* 33 (2) March 1972 119-121, James Anderson describes how Library of Congress proof-slips and a Xerox 914 copier can be economically utilized in the cataloguing operations of a library. A break-even formula is derived and an example of its use is given from data gathered at Arkansas State University.

Xerox Bibliographics advertise a commercial service for conversion of card catalogs into 'Xerox book catalogs'.

Photography: The increasing availability of authoritative cataloguing data enshrined in the volumes of the LC catalogues, *National union catalog, British national bibliography* and BM *General catalogue* and many other sources, has led to a search for the 'cataloguer's camera' which, ideally, would instantly photograph and enlarge entries found in such sources. These photographic copies could then be duplicated in order to produce 'sets' for insertion in the catalogue. The US Council on Library Resources investigated the production of such a camera shortly after it was set up in 1956, but while some progress was made the camera failed to materialise, apparently on the grounds that perhaps too much was being required of the device *ie* it was required to transfer the tracings at the foot of the LC entries on to the headings of the reproduced cards. In the 1960s, however, a suitable camera, the Polaroid Cu-5, was developed and used (at the University of Vermont, for instance, see H Oustinoff 'University of Vermont uses a Polaroid CU-5 to speed book processing' *Library resources and technical services* 11 (4) Fall 1967 474-478). D Kennedy reports ('Cataloguers' cameras' *Microdocumentation* 10 (1) 1971 6-9) that this is the only commercially produced camera. He notes that its main disadvantage is its high cost and shows that 'home-built' cameras, while not offering instant copy as the Cu-5 does, are not so expensive. Kennedy points to the 35mm reflex equipment in use at UKAEA Risley and the photographic equipment developed at Arizona University Library and the State University of New York.

The spirit duplicator (hectography): An 'art' paper master with a special backing sheet of 'transfer' or carbon paper is used to prepare a typewritten master. The master is then clipped to the duplicator, and by damping copy with spirit as both elements are passed under a rotary drum an image is transferred from master to copy under pressure. *Features*: Economy of materials, speedy processing and drying of copy, 'masking' to give alteration of headings is possible, economic for quite few copies and capable of reproducing 150 or more copies on card before the dye is exhausted. Two particular disadvantages are that the copy is not as 'crisp' as in other methods, and that the image will fade if long exposed to strong sunlight (although there is little danger of this in catalogue files).

Offset lithography: Provides a number of ways (typing, photography, xerography) of producing the master on a metal or plastic-surfaced mat, employing the lithographic principle of the ink adhering only to the greasy image and being repelled elsewhere on the damped plate. The image is transferred to a rubber blanket and thence to the copy. Excellent, quickly drying copies are obtainable and long runs are possible. But the method is fairly expensive in materials and more so in equipment. Even the smallest offset-litho machine is much more expensive than other types of duplicator and more complex in maintenance.

Addressing machines: They may use as masters embossed metal plates, stencils, or hectographic paper, and have the advantage that since they were designed to mechanise the addressing of envelopes, their printing area and ancillary printing equipment approaches that required for standard sizes of catalogue cards. They have proved capable of adaptation for card reproduction, with certain limitations regarding rigidity of layout, number of lines of print available on the master; but a main feature of the addressing machine systems—the ability to store the master indefinitely for continual re-use—provides no essential benefit in most kinds of libraries.

Some copying methods employ combinations of photographic or xerographic processes, microfilm, multilith, automatic typewriters, etc, and much research and development proceeds. The possibility of producing cards from MARC or other machine readable tapes, which has already been mentioned, should also be renoted here. (See, for instance, 'MARC-produced cards: production of cards from MARC-compatible cataloguing tapes before computer input', by Ruth Irvine and Gloria Nicholas *Catalogue and index* (25) Spring 1972 8-9.)

The pamphlet by Philip S Pargeter *The reproduction of catalogue cards* (London, LA 1960) provides basic reading on this subject. The ALA Library Technology Project *Catalogue card reproduction: report on a study conducted by George Fry & Associates* (Chicago, ALA 1965) comprehensively examines and costs some thirteen processes and finds that on a basis of costs, libraries who require cards for 1,000-2,000 titles a year should consider 1 Printed cards, 2 Typing, 3 Reproduction by fluid or stencil duplication. Larger libraries (2,000-9,000 card sets per year) should consider stencil duplication with full-size equipment, offset duplication, and electrostatic copying equipment. An article based on the LTP study is J H Treyz ' Equipment and methods in catalog card reproduction' *Library resources* 8 (3) Summer 1964 267-278.

Two more recent articles are: 'Catalogue card reproduction: a survey of equipment and a bibliography', by Helen M Jenkins *Library information bulletin* (17) 1972 2-24, which is arranged under the following headings: Duplicators (stencil); Duplicators (spirit); Addressing machines; Embossed plate; Spirit; Stencil; Offset printing machines; Automatic typewriters; Xerography; Printed card services; Cataloguer's cameras, and 'Comparative card production methods', by Ann Craig Turner *Library resources and technical services* 16 (3) Summer 1972 347-358.

Central cataloguing agencies and the use of printed cards

No one is more conscious of the duplication of effort and wasteful repetition than the cataloguer establishing the entry for a new, and perhaps difficult book, who knows that hundreds of other cataloguers, using the same codes and classification schedules, are probably doing precisely the same thing at approximately the same time. This is a paradoxical situation which can be avoided by the creation of a central authority where the operation of classifying and cataloguing of books can be done, and the entries then made available to libraries throughout the country.

Library of Congress

The Library of Congress, as a by-product of cataloguing its acquisitions, has made copies of its printed cards available for purchase and use by libraries since 1901. The cards carry LC and DC class numbers, subject heading tracings, and an LC serial number. The serial numbers are carried in the US trade bibliographies—Wilson's *Cumulative book index,* Bowker's *Publisher's weekly* and *Book publishing record,* and using these numbers US librarians can order card sets from LC at the same time as they order the titles from the bookseller.

The tremendous demands made upon the LC card division made automation essential. Such a system, involving direct optical scanning techniques to sort orders according to card stock numbers and the automatic printing of cards, has now been introduced. This system will provide a faster, more accurate and economical service (see 'Development of the Card Automated Reproduction and Distribution System (CARDS) at the Library of Congress', by Stephen R Salmon. In *Proceedings of the 1969 clinic on library applications of data processing, April 27-29, 1969* edited by Dewey E Carroll University of Illinois, Graduate School of Library Science 1970 98-113).

Commercial services in the US

There are several commercial cataloguing services in the US, including: *US Reprint Service, Xerox Bibliographics,* and *H W Wilson,* all of which supply sets of cards; the *Micrographic Catalog Retrieval System,* a microfiche service from which cards can be produced by reader/printers; and the *Card Mate Publication System,* which provides reproductions of LC proofsheets. Commercial services are compared with that provided by LC in 'Commercial cataloguing', by Elizabeth A Neal *Law library journal* 64 (1) February 1971 23-28.

British National Bibliography

The UK had to wait until 1950 to see the beginnings of a similar central service to that made available by the Library of Congress. The British National Bibliography, originally working from the books received by legal deposit in the British Museum and later from those received by the Agency for the Copyright Libraries, produces a weekly printed list with entries classified and arranged by the latest edition of DC (prior to 1971, BNB used the 14th edition of DC with adjustments from later editions and notational modifications). Author/title indexes are provided and a separate subject index (using PRECIS—see p 126) is included in the last issue of each month. There are now two four monthly cumulations per annum, followed by an annual volume and usually, except for 1965-7, five yearly cumulations are issued.

A printed card service was commenced in 1956, and for material recorded from the first of January that year, cards could be purchased from BNB, using the BNB serial number (or now the SBN—see below) cited in the entry. The cards carry DC numbers. Production of the cards is automatic, and cards are forwarded by return of post, compared with a LC delivery time (quoted by Neal in the article cited above) of 3-6 weeks. However, due note should be taken of the complexity and much wider coverage of the LC service.

Certain categories of material are omitted from BNB, *eg* maps, some government publications such as parliamentary papers, cheap novelettes, reprints etc. BNB found it necessary in 1962 to exclude US publications issued through UK outlets. (It should be noted that LC cards, since they represent the library's acquisitions, cover much foreign material, while BNB cards are essentially a by-product of a national bibliography.) A J Wells has described the card service in ' Printed catalogue cards ' *Journal of documentation* 13 (2) 1957 67-71. The method of producing the cards has, however, altered somewhat since this article was written. The stencils from which the cards are printed are now mechanically produced using the BNB in its initial 'punched tape' machine readable form.

The BNB from its inception has displayed a remarkable capacity for making quite sweeping changes in some of its practices, a capacity which might not be expected to be found in a body committed to producing a national bibliographical service and a national cataloguing service. Some examples of this are to be found in its switch from orthodox DC numbers to applying ' verbal extensions ' after the arbitrary sign ' [1] ' in 1951, and later again, in 1960, grafting an alpha-numerical supplementary notation onto DC numbers, to achieve more exact subject specification by means of this classification. Such changes were not greeted always with universal applause by BNB users.

Some of the more important changes put into operation in recent years have been:

1968 Adoption of AACR.
Tracings given at the foot of each entry in the weekly list.
Inclusion of the SBN in the imprint of each entry.

1971 Adoption of standard (*ie* latest) edition of DC.
Chain indexing replaced by a rotated (or shunted) indexing system known as PRECIS (PREserved Context Indexing System).

1972 Adoption of ISBD (see p 95).

SBN—Standard Book Number

The idea of numbering books is not new, but what is an entirely new concept is that a unique and non-changeable number should be allocated to *every* book. The need for such a system became urgent because of the increased use of computers. Numeric codes representing specific books facilitate machine handling of bibliographic information.

The code is in three parts. In the number 85157 109 3, for example, the 85157 relates to the publisher, Bingley, the 109 identifies the particular title, *An introduction to chain indexing*, and the 3 is a 'check' digit which enables the computer to verify whether a number is valid or not.

The ISBN (International Standard Book Number) has a further preceding 'group identifier' which shows, for international use, the area from which the number originated. The above example would be preceded by a 0, *ie* 0 85157 109 3, which stands for the American, British, Canadian and Australian group. Such numbers are extremely useful where the international exchange of bibliographic data is concerned. A useful pamphlet is the Standard Book Numbering Agency's *Standard book numbering* (London, 1967). David Whitaker deals briefly with 'International Standard Book Numbering' in the *Penrose annual* for 1970 p 209-212.

Complementing the International Standard Book Number is the International Standard Serial Number (ISSN), a unique number which identifies a particular serial title. This is a seven digit number plus a check digit, which is divided into two groups of four digits and should always be preceded by the letters ISSN, *eg*

ISSN   1234.5672

The ISSN is managed by the International Centre of the International Serials Data System (ISDS) in Paris (see *International cataloguing* 1 (4) October/December 1972 4-6).

PRECIS

When it was decided to produce the BNB by computerised methods, investigation showed that chain indexing could not easily be 'automated'. This was mainly due to the fact that the method is directly related to a classification scheme and all such schemes have faults (non-hierarchical notation, lack of hospitality and flexibility, etc) which make the computerisation of 'chain' such a complicated programming procedure as to be impractical. The special research team set up to examine techniques for adding subject data to the MARC record soon came to the conclusion that what was required was a new type of indexing system, to be completely independent of any particular classification scheme. Strongly influenced by the work of the Classification Research Group, PRECIS began to be developed.

At first, PRECIS was referred to as a 'rotated' index, but later the term 'shunted' was used. Unlike chain indexing, the 'context' is preserved at all entry points and the acronym actually stands for PREserved Context Indexing System.

Each index entry basically consists of two lines, *ie*

| LEAD | | Qualifier |

| Display |

On the top line concepts become progressively more 'general' and on the bottom line progressively more 'specific'. To take an example, the subject 'the plating of spokes in bicycle wheels' would first of all be 'analysed' and this analysis would produce a 'string' of cencepts, *ie*

Bicycles   Wheels   Spokes   Plating

These concepts are allocated symbols known as 'relational operators' and from these each concept is given a 'manipulation' code. These codes indicate to the computer how to manipulate the terms to form the index. The concepts in the above example would be allocated a 'standard' coding which would result in a 'standard' set of entries, *ie*

126

Project MARC

In 1966, the Library of Congress announced that one important part of its automation programme 'a project to test the feasibility of the central production and distribution of machine-readable catalogue data' was under way and Project MARC (MAchine Readable Catalog) came into being. Towards the end of 1966 it was distributing weekly tapes (each of which carried machine-readable data for about eight hundred titles) to the sixteen selected libraries participating in the experiment. The libraries receiving the magnetic tape processed it through their own computing facilities, the most common requirement being that of the production of catalogue cards. The pilot project was limited to cataloguing data for current English-language monographs and by the end of the test period, eight months after commencement, the complete tape carried some sixteen thousand entries.

Even before the end of the pilot project, work had begun on a MARC II format and this became fully operational in December, 1967, with about fifty libraries receiving tapes on a subscription basis. In this same year the BNB was able, by virtue of an OSTI grant, to commence work on the development of a MARC system in Britain. By September 1968, tapes were being produced and, in May 1969, a regular MARC service began with the distribution of tapes to fifteen selected libraries, which tested various methods of use. This experimental service ended in 1970 and latest figures show that there are now more than double that number of libraries in the UK making some use of MARC. A report on the period September, 1970 to March, 1973 has been issued: *BNB/MARC project* ... (London, BNB 1973).

MARC I had certain limitations, it used, for example, fixed fields, which meant that any constituent element of a catalogue entry could not exceed a certain length. MARC II made the record much more flexible. Variable length fields are used and each entry includes a full standard description based upon AACR and/or ISBD. Records are arranged on the tape according to the SBN and each record is capable of containing a vast number of compounds, *eg* price of book, LC subject heading, index entries by PRECIS, etc. Any one element may be used as a means of approach and it is, therefore, possible to create different forms of output.

E H C Driver suggested at a British seminar held in 1969 that MARC could stand for Multi Access Research Catalogue (Seminar on the UK MARC Project, *University of Southampton, 1969 . . . Proceedings* . . . edited by A E Jeffreys and T D Wilson (Newcastle, Oriel Press for the LA Cataloguing and Indexing Group 1970 p 56). This might in fact be a more suitable translation of the acronym, for MARC now spreads its influence across the whole spectrum of library activity, including selection, ordering, cataloguing, information retrieval, production of bibliographies, etc. Coward has suggested ('BNB and computers' *Library Association record* 70 (8) August 1968 198-202) that the answer to the question 'What can I do with a MARC tape?' might vary from its use in processing orders for booksellers to its use in a computerised 'store' which allows individual access to information by means of personal consoles.

MARC continues to develop, and the description of the MARC format for monographs has reached a fifth edition (US *Library of Congress. MARC Development Office Books: a MARC format; specifications for magnetic tapes containing catalog records for books* 5th ed Washington, 1972). Formats for other forms of library materials such as films, maps, manuscripts, music, sound recordings and serials have been or are being developed. Details of these and other relevant publications are included in the bibliography contained in the brief but very useful *Information on the MARC system,* also prepared by the MARC Development Office (2nd ed 1972).

MARC is no longer confined to Britain and America. Countries such as Australia, Canada, France, Germany, Netherlands, Scandinavia and South Africa have agreed to work to the same MARC format standard.

In America, the LC 'seems increasingly responsive to the consumers of MARC' (*Library resources and technical services* 17 (2) Spring 1973 182) and the subscription price has been stabilised at $1,000 yearly.* The RECON project, which was an attempt to analyse the problems of large scale conversion to machine readable form of retrospective catalogue records, has however been suspended and those records so far converted have been placed on sale.

Despite the suspension of the RECON project, 'the use of machine-readable catalog records in the USA has increased with the corresponding rise of the number of records in the MARC data bases' (Library of Congress *Information bulletin* 33 (2) January 11 1974 A-11).

* For note on cost of MARC in UK see end of chapter.

notable experiment by LC cataloguers aided by a grant from the Council on Library Resources. Cataloguers worked from advance proof-sheets and from bibliographical information supplied by the publishers before publication. The cataloguers found the data difficult to handle in form and content, only about half of the 300 publishers invited co-operated and there were many complaints of inconvenience and disruption of schedules. It was found that LC would need more money, more staff and at least three regional centres to operate the system properly, and the rather disappointing conclusion of the Library of Congress *The cataloging-in-source experiment: a report* (Washington, LC, 1960) was that the programme ' could not be justified from the viewpoint of financing, technical considerations, or utility.' Comprehensive reviews of the report appeared in *Library resources* 4 (4) 1960 269-284.

Despite this abandonment, there was an ever increasing awareness of the great advantages of such a system and the economics that it could achieve. However, a further ten years was to elapse before it was decided that the project, now called 'cataloging-in-publication' (CIP) was worth further investigation. The new CIP project began in 1971 as a three year pilot project.

There has since been a spate of articles dealing with CIP. Three of these, tracing its history, appear in *Library resources and technical services* 15 (1) Winter 1971. Verner W Clapp refers to CIP as possibly the 'greatest invention since the title page' in *Wilson library bulletin* 46 (4) December 1971 348-359. By 1972, however, doubts were again being expressed as to whether it would succeed, and Henry Wingate reports ('Cataloging-in-Publication: problems and prospects' *Library resources and technical services* 16 (4) Fall 1972 423-432) that the current programme faces the same difficulties which resulted in the failure of the earlier 1958-9 experiment. Wingate states that librarians will need to demonstrate the programme's use and his sentiments are echoed by Margaret Brown, 'Librarians must be vociferous if they wish to keep CIP' 'Cataloging-in-Publication: will it succeed?' *PLA bulletin* 27 (3) May 1972 113-120.

There are presently (January 1974) over 500 publishers participating in the CIP programme. 26,000 titles have been processed since the project began, including 1,400 titles cooperatively catalogued by LC with the National Library of Medicine. Weekly receipts average between 250 and 350 titles.

133

It is not only in the USA that cataloguing-in-source experiments have been carried out. In Russia some of the large publishing houses have supplied a model cataloguing card in some of their books (see Eleanor Buist 'Steps towards cataloguing at source in the USSR' *Wilson library bulletin* 44 (10) June 1970 1033-1039) and Brazil (see 'Cataloguing-in-Publication 2: a Brazilian short experience', by Regina Carneiro *International cataloguing* 1 (2) April-June 1972 5-6) has also introduced it. In the UK, the BNB is apparently committed to mount a cataloguing in advance of publication project in 1974.

Shared cataloguing

Literally this means co-operation between libraries to 'share' the cataloguing load but the term actually came into being to describe one of the most dramatic and far reaching developments in centralised cataloguing which was briefly and quietly announced in 'Report on a conference on shared cataloging, London, January 13, 1966' *Library of Congress information bulletin* 25 (7) February 1966 *appendix*. Representatives of LC, BM, BNB, Bibliothèque Nationale and several other European national libraries had agreed that LC should receive for cataloguing purposes the entries in the various national bibliographies, securing a copy of the listings as soon as possible, even in advance of the publication of the national bibliography.

Behind this agreement lay the work of many American librarians, not least that of the Shared Cataloging Committee of the American Association of Research Libraries. Set up in 1963 to consider the problem that almost half the acquisitions in the major US libraries were not covered by LC printed cards, the committee decided that the answer was not to be found in co-operative cataloguing but in *centralised cataloguing* with Library of Congress as the central source. The representatives of the committee, supported by other library organisations and the Library of Congress, succeeded in having Title II-c written into the US Higher Education Act of 1965 whereby (NPAC) the National Program for Acquisitions and Cataloging, otherwise known as the 'Shared Cataloging Program', came into being. Title II-c authorises the Library of Congress to become globally comprehensive in its acquisitions of scholarly materials, and to provide cataloguing data for such acquisitions *promptly* after receipt, distributing such data by printed cards and by any other means.

With the necessary funds available, LC acted swiftly in response to its widened role and responsibilities. As early as June 1967 there were Shared Cataloguing Offices in most of the principal cities in Europe, one in South America and one in Africa and the programme continued to expand. These offices, working in conjunction with the national sources of bibliographic data, acquire the descriptive copy of catalogue entries as soon as possible, carry out preliminary conversion work so that the entry will conform in heading and some other details with LC practice, select and acquire the appropriate books and ship books and cards by air to the Shared Cataloging Division at LC. LC accept as much as possible of the original entry, adding such details as LC and DC class numbers and LC subject headings, and publishes the final printed card entry as rapidly as it can.

To the cataloguers and subject bibliographers who are aware of the painfully slow and almost reluctant acceptance of the ancient and historic arguments for centralised bibliographic control in the quite modest local or national contexts, the swift and near-effortless emergence of LC as the international centre for the collection, formulation and distribution of bibliographical information and cataloguing data may seem almost miraculous. Representing as it does the agreement of so many librarians, libraries and agencies on an international basis and linked with the possibility of interchange of the cataloguing information by means of newer media, shared cataloguing offers immediate benefits of international library co-operation in the vital area of cataloguing. Papers given at the 33rd session of the IFLA General Council, Toronto, August 1967 and published in *Libri* 17 (4) 1967 270-304 give a most complete account of the Shared Cataloguing Program. In particular, J E Skipper ' International implications of the Shared Cataloguing Program: introductory statement pp 270-275 ' gives an historical account of the development of the idea, while J G Lorenz ' International implications of the Shared Cataloging Program: planning for bibliographic control ' pp 276-284 describes in some detail the operations at both the Library of Congress and the offices abroad.

A great deal of progress has been made since these articles were written. From the beginning of the project in 1966 to 1973, participating libraries in 24 NPAC shared cataloguing countries had reported a total of well over 800,000 titles for which catalogue data was not available at a first search. A high percentage of these had in fact already been received by LC or were already on order but these reports resulted in orders being placed for some 170,000 titles not previously acquired.

From the outset the programme attracted considerable attention outside the US and it has been pointed out by some writers that 'shared cataloguing' refers to only one part of the scheme. NPAC can be considered as a first step, and a major step, towards the achievement of a system of universal bibliographic control (UBC).

An idea of the importance attached to shared cataloguing by various countries can be gleaned from papers contributed to the Meetings of Experts on Shared Cataloguing organised by the Council of Europe's Committee for Higher Education and Research and held in Strasbourg in June, 1972.

The interplay that exists between 'shared', 'co-operative' and 'centralized' cataloguing should be noted. Shared cataloguing implies co-operation and today co-operative cataloguing often involves the use of some centralised service.

Limited cataloguing

A cataloguing code will prescribe the amount of descriptive detail to be recorded in respect of a book or document and, in appropriate cases, indicate which added entries should be made under other headings. But the codes cannot consider such factors as the relative importance in a particular library of a two-page document and a scholarly treatise, between ephemeral material which will quickly go out of date and soon be discarded, and other material considered to be of permanent value. Librarians, however, faced with the continuing high cost of cataloguing and with the not infrequent situation of an ever-increasing volume of acquisitions outstripping the capability of cataloguers to deal with it, have sometimes sought an answer to these problems in the policy of limited cataloguing, *ie* by *reducing* the amount of *cataloguing* that is carried out. This may be achieved in several ways:

1 By simplifying the entry heading, *eg* author's surname and initials only, no forenames.

2 By reducing the descriptive part of the entry. This may range from a modest decision not to include a full collation statement to the drastic reduction of an entry to a form just barely capable of identifying the item, *eg* short title, edition and date. Limitations of this nature are practised to a certain extent in most libraries.

3 By eliminating certain added entries, *eg* no added title entries.

4 By applying any one or more of the above to certain kinds of material only, *eg* fiction, children's books, pamphlets, etc.

5 By omitting catalogue entries altogether for some categories of material, *eg* maps, or material consisting of groups of documents (HMSO, UN, UNESCO) which may be considered to be 'self-indexing', especially if the collection is fairly comprehensive and a marked-up checklist or printed catalogue is separately available.

1, 2 and 3 are sometimes referred to as *simplified* cataloguing. When simplified cataloguing is applied only to certain sections of a library's stock, as in 4, or such sections are not catalogued at all, as in 5, then this process may be referred to as *selective* cataloguing. It should be pointed out, however, that the two terms tend to overlap and previous attempts at defining them have led to some confusion. The generic term 'limited' cataloguing is to be preferred.

In support of such policies it can be said that the range of materials acquired in most libraries and the varying values thereof, often seem to indicate the necessity for differential treatment; and again, any policy which tends to speed the process of cataloguing and thus makes material, to whatever extent, more quickly available, seems desirable. However, this has to be balanced against the possibility that a cataloguing system which creates differential treatments in the work-flow can be uneconomic also. For example, sorting the books and documents into categories can be time-consuming, and applying different rules to different categories may be equally as expensive as applying uniform treatment to all material. There is the added danger that by simplifying too much, some bibliographical work may be removed from the shoulders of the cataloguers, simply to be placed on those of other library staff.

The Library of Congress policy of 'limited cataloguing' included a division of books and documents into four categories, each receiving differential treatment according to the rules given in *Cataloging rules . . . additions and changes* (1949-58) p 73-76. F Bernice Field, chairman of the ALA Descriptive Cataloging

Committee, briefly reported on the cessation of the policy in August 1963 in *Library resources* 8 (3) Summer 1964 301 stating simply that 'A Study of their experience of eleven years with the rules and of comments received from card subscribers and others led them to the conclusion that a single set of rules should be in force for all publications'. An interesting account of fairly extreme simplified *and* selective cataloguing is described in R K Engelbarts and H D Williams ' Brieflisting: a method for controlling catalogue arrears ' *Library resources* 9 (2) Spring 1965 191-199 whereby some 60,000 backlog items had *one* card bearing author's name, shelf number and reduced photo-facsimile of the title page inserted in the catalogue. D Benson ' Instant cataloguing ' *Canadian library* 22 (6) May 1966 419-421 describes a one-entry system with simplified title-page-available data transcribed by non-professional cataloguers, headings being taken from LC catalogues and other sources, employed in the National Library of Canada for several hundred thousand un-catalogued items.

Bakewell (p 216-219) notes some further 'case studies' of limited cataloguing; for example at the University of Aston limitations include 'the use of initials instead of full names of authors regard-less of what appears on the title page. Trade catalogues are simply arranged alphabetically by manufacturers, and British Standards are not catalogued since they are retrievable via the *British Stan-dards yearbook*. Inaugural lectures from various universities are boxed and arranged alphabetically by name of institution, and publications of political parties and such bodies as the Fabian Society are catalogued collectively and held in boxes with appro-priate class numbers. Building Research Station publications are also catalogued as a group; they are given added entries under author but not subject.' Practices such as *Bakewell* describes are widespread.

Analytical cataloguing

Analytical entries can be made for individual *parts* of a book or other item (even down to a significant paragraph or illustration contained therein if considered important enough) under *author* or *subject* or *title* of the part analysed and may be made sometimes under all three headings.

Analytical cataloguing is frequently necessary in the case of

has declined in most library catalogues since the more stately days when an unhurried cataloguer dealt with a gentle flow of acquisitions. This decline was obviously due, however, to economic factors rather than to an acceptance that annotation was no longer required. When annotation is still included in entries, these same economic factors stipulate that it must necessarily be limited in length, about thirty words being generally considered acceptable. Most desirably, they should concentrate on the factual, giving such details as 1 author's status or authority in relation to his subject; 2 the level of treatment; 3 the type of reader at whom the work is aimed. Critical or evaluative annotations which would present the reader with the cataloguer's assessment of the importance, value and merit of the work are usually to be avoided, if only for the obvious reason that, unless the cataloguer is a subject specialist, such judgements can hardly be valid. (One method of overcoming the latter difficulty is sometimes to be found in the use of quotations from authoritative reviews, but even this method, as in publishers' blurbs, can result in bias.)

Although annotation in catalogue entries is practised less nowadays, a tendency accelerated by the brief, computer generated entry, annotation in subject booklists and reading lists must still be regarded as extremely useful. Such material aims at creating interest in special subjects, or is designed for a special group of readers such as children (the LC printed cards for children's literature, the issue of which began in 1966, carried a brief annotation). Here there is less need to avoid personal comment or criticism, the purpose is to *stimulate*, although care should still be taken that remarks are not made that might be better left to the subject specialist.

A survey of catalogue annotation was reported by P Ward 'Annotation in public library catalogues: British practice and policy', *Library Association record* 64 (6) June 1962 208-212. *Bakewell* (chapter 9) is also well worth reading on the subject.

Filing

Whatever policies are adopted and whatever method is used to obtain, produce or reproduce entries for the catalogue, eventually these entries must be filed into the catalogue sequence. This is not such a simple operation as it might appear for there are many problems. For instance a basic decision must be taken as to whether 'word by word' or 'letter by letter', *eg*:

Word by word	Letter by letter
South	South
South Australia	Southampton
South pole	South Australia
Southampton	Southey
Southey	South pole

There are also difficulties with regard to initials, abbreviations, hyphenated words etc, and decisions must be taken as to the arrangement to be used under an author's name or within the subdivisions of a complex subject.

There are several codes of filing rules, the best known of which is probably the *ALA rules for filing catalog cards* edited by Pauline Seely (Chicago, American Library Association 2nd ed 1968). Others include that of the Library of Congress (*Filing rules for the dictionary catalogs of the Library of Congress* Washington 1956), which is based on Cutter, and the simple *British standard 1749: 1969*.

Bakewell (chapter 11) provides an excellent review of filing methods and the varying approaches used by different codes.

The application of the computer to cataloguing and indexing has presented new problems with relation to filing, for how can a machine know that St is filed as Saint, Dr as Doctor, etc. In the UK, a Working Party on Computer Filing Rules was set up in 1966 and its report delivered 1972. The entire issue of *Catalogue and index* (27) Autumn 1972 is devoted to a presentation of the working party's findings.

Cataloguing in different kinds of library

It has been the practice in some previous books on cataloguing to include a section on the varying methods and techniques employed in different kinds of library. However, for a number of reasons, it no longer seems necessary to stress such differences; these reasons include:

1 The present trend towards standardisation at local, national and international levels.

2 The increased use of mechanisation, which has meant that

techniques which were once the prerogative of the 'special' library are now also used by other types of library.

3 Mechanisation has brought with it improved centralised services. This has led to a radical change of attitude on the part of certain libraries. Many university libraries in the UK, for instance, in direct contrast to their previous unwillingness to make use of centralised services, now subscribe to MARC.

4 Mechanisation has also been mainly responsible for increased co-operation between libraries of various types. The BLCMP (see p 31 is an outstanding example of such co-operation.

5 The use of automation has led in some cases to a reduction in the number of staff required to manage the cataloguing department. It is therefore possible for a large automated library system to employ fewer cataloguers than a smaller system which still uses manual methods. As noted on p 140, however, staff could be redeployed to other tasks such as analytical cataloguing and indexing.

6 In the UK, the reorganisation of local government has meant the amalgamation of certain authorities into much larger units and municipal library systems now have problems similar to those that have had to be faced by the counties for many years. There is, for example, the forming of large central collections and the setting up of a headquarters which will control a widely scattered array of branches and mobiles. In addition, this reorganisation has brought new problems of integration of differing methods which, in the cataloguing field, include variant physical and inner forms of catalogue. The previous experiences of the London boroughs can provide some guidance in the handling of these problems. W S H Ashmore 'Cataloguing, classification and book provision in the new London boroughs' *Assistant librarian* 59 (4) April 1966 74-77 discusses the problems of classification and cataloguing in the amalgamation of systems which had previously used various editions of DC and the Brown ' Subject classification ', and employed both classified and dictionary forms of catalogue. He considers that the best hope for the problems of these larger bibliographic service areas may lie in computerised catalogue systems. F Bennett ' Mergers and catalogues ' *Library Association record* 70 (4) April 1968 100-102 describes the integration of three separate cataloguing systems in the new London Borough of Tower Hamlets, finding it necessary to carry out conversion opera-

tions in a more conventional manner before computerisation can be considered. Bennett expands upon this theme in *Cataloguing in practice: the organisation of book acquisition in libraries* (London, Bingley: Hamden, Conn, Linnet 1972).

However, despite the above trends, there must obviously remain certain aspects of catalogue provision which are unique to the particular type of library. Some of these will be related to the user.

The public library serves all manner of users from children to students doing advanced research. A selective cataloguing policy may therefore be applied involving perhaps simplified cataloguing in the children's department and full cataloguing in the reference library.

Conversely, the readership in a university library will be much more restricted, ranging from undergraduates requiring material for their courses to postgraduates doing highly specialised research. Here there will be the problem of cataloguing a much larger proportion of special subject, including foreign, material.

There are so many different types of 'special' library that it is almost impossible to make generalised comments about them. In most such libraries, however, the clientele will be specialists in the subject field covered and the emphasis is more on the provision of an information service. Acquisitions may include a relatively small proportion of books and a high proportion of periodicals, abstracting literature and reports, etc. Many special libraries use post-coordinate and computerised techniques rather than conventional cataloguing methods.

Four chapters in *Piggott* give accounts of practice in various types of libraries (chapter 9, S J Butcher 'Municipal libraries'; chapter 10, L Paulin 'County libraries'; chapter 11, R S Mortimer 'University libraries'; chapter 12 L Jolley 'Special libraries), but it sould be remembered that this work is now somewhat dated. *Bakewell* (p 222-229) provides a brief but useful survey of methods.

J Friedman and A Jeffreys 'Cataloguing and classification in British university libraries, a survey of practices and procedures' *Journal of documentation* 23 (3) September 1967 179-272 (also separately published by Sheffield University Postgraduate School of Librarianship, 1967) report in detail and depth on practice in fifty one libraries which returned an elaborate questionnaire. The general picture emerging is, not unexpectedly, one of great

'new terms or class numbers are added reluctantly'). This group would include 'conventional classification and cataloguing', for example the *Dewey decimal classification* and *Subject headings used in the dictionary catalogs of the Library of Congress.* Such lists of subject headings as the latter may be described as using 'controlled' or 'artificial' language. Bourne also includes in this group Calvin Mooers 'descriptor' system. His descriptor* is a broad heading that stands for an idea or concept, but is most carefully chosen to suit the needs of the particular group of index users and is thus tailored precisely to their search vocabulary. Mooers describes the basis of his Descriptors and how they are chosen in a paper 'The indexing language of an information retrieval system in W Simonton *ed Information retrieval today* (Minneapolis, University of Minnesota, 1963) p 21-36, asserting that the list of thesaurus of Descriptors for any chosen subject field should not exceed two hundred and fifty.

A 'fixed' classification or indexing scheme usually represents the particular viewpoint of the person or persons who developed it. It is possible, however, to produce schemes which do not restrict the indexing of a particular item to a single approach or point of view. Such schemes comprise Bourne's *third* group and included in it are faceted classification schemes involving *analysis* and *synthesis,* such as the colon classification, UDC and more recent specialised schemes such as the *London education classification.* Certain recent specialised lists of subject headings (referred to as 'thesauri' or 'controlled vocabularies') have also been compiled using classificatory techniques. One outstanding example of a special scheme is the English Electric *Thesaurofacet,* which is an interactive combined thesaurus and faceted classification. Another type of faceted classification is the semantic code, developed at Western Reserve University *c* 1950. This indexing technique uses 'semantic factoring', whereby terms are broken down into a set of fundamental concepts. A thermometer is a *device* for *measuring temperature.* Each 'semantic factor' is allocated a code for 'machine searching', as the system is geared to computer retrieval. This system has been described by B C Vickery 'The structure of semantic coding: a review' *American documentation* 10 (3) July 1959 234-241, and also by instigators J W Perry and A Kent *Tools for machine litera-*

* The term 'descriptor' now appears to be used loosely for any type of subject heading.

149

ture searching: semantic code dictionary: equipment: procedures
(New York, London, Interscience 1958).

This type of grouping, which has also been used by writers other than Bourne, is helpful to the beginner in that it assists in the identification and understanding of the principles underlying various systems. Nevertheless it still presents certain problems of overlap and ambiguity. Bourne himself recognises that in the first group, indexes may require 'enrichment' by the addition of terms not used in the text and thus the 'natural' language element is removed and also the simplicity of such systems which permits of untrained personnel performing the indexing operation. Similarly a post-coordinate index may make use of lists of subject headings, in which case it would rightfully belong in group two. In fact, because post-coordinate indexes may be approached from *any* viewpoint they could also be included in group three.

Key-word indexing

'Key-word' systems basically rely on the selection as index entries of the more important terms from a document's title. These are printed out with the addition of some of the preceding and following words to show the context of the key-word, *eg*

The BINOMIAL theorem

Primary EDUCATION

GYMNASTICS for schools

The teaching of MATHEMATICS in universities

PRIMARY education

Gymnastics for SCHOOLS

The TEACHING of mathematics in
universities

The binomial THEOREM

The teaching of mathematics in UNIVERSITIES

In automated systems, words not required as index entry points are placed on a 'stop' list and the computer is programmed to ignore them. Words such as 'the', 'for', 'of' and 'in', *ie* articles and prepositions, are obvious candidates for such treatment but any word considered unnecessary as an indexing term can be included.

The above example illustrates KWIC (Key-Word *In* Context) Indexing. Another similar method is KWOC (Key-Word *Out-of* Context), which is illustrated below:

BINOMIAL	The binomial theorem
EDUCATION	Primary education
GYMNASTICS	Gymnastics for schools
MATHEMATICS	The teaching of mathematics in universities etc.

Some indexes are referred to as KWAC (Key-Word *And* Context), which is perhaps difficult to distinguish from KWOC.

Key-word indexing was introduced by H P Luhn, who describes the system in 'Key-word-in-context index for technical literature' *American documentation* 11 (4) October 1960 288-295. A feature of such indexes is that they require the minimum of intellectual effort and they are, therefore, eminently suitable for mechanisation. The basic idea is not, of course, a new one. Crestadoro used it in the nineteenth century and the inevitable disadvantages then noted are still applicable. The major one is that titles often do not convey the subject matter of documents.

Some key-word indexes have an additional element in that author's names are also indexed. Examples are WADEX (Word and Author inDEX) and AKWIC (Author and Key-Word in Context Index). The former is considered in 'Wadex: a new tool in literature searching', by E A Ripperger, H Wooster and S Juhasz *Mechanical engineering* March 1964 45-50 and the latter (which is a compromise between KWIC and WADEX in that the author is included but each entry occupies only one line) in a brief pamphlet by S Juhasz *AKWIC* (San Antonio, Texas, Applied mechanics reviews 1969).

It is possible that the efficiency of key-word indexing could be increased as the result of research by Dr Anthony Petrarca at the Ohio State University. Dr Petrarca has developed a technique called 'Double-KWIC co-ordinate indexing'. The normal KWIC index only provides access via a single concept but the Double-KWIC technique facilitates speedy co-ordination with other concepts. This is achieved by taking a word or phrase that would normally appear in the KWIC index column, extracting this word as a main term and identifying its original location in the complete context by an asterisk. The remaining context is then rotated to create an ordered list of *subordinate* entries under the main term, *ie*:

NOMENCLATURE

FLUORINATED MOLECULES	THE * OF HIGHLY
HIGHLY FLUORINATED MOLECULES	THE * OF
MOLECULES	THE * OF HIGHLY FLUORINATED

As the index expands, it would begin to take on the following appearance:

NOMENCLATURE
BIOCHEMICAL *   THE ORGANISATION AND FUNCTIONING OF
CARBOHYDRATE *
CHEMISTRY   THE * OF ORGANIC
FLUORINATED MOLECULES   THE * OF HIGHLY
FUNCTIONING OF BIOCHEMICAL *   THE ORGANISATION AND
HIGHLY FLUORINATED MOLECULES   THE * OF
MOLECULES   THE * OF HIGHLY FLUORINATED
ORGANIC CHEMISTRY   THE * OF
ORGANISATION AND FUNCTIONING OF BIOCHEMICAL *   THE

Dr Petrarca and Michael Lay report on *The Double-KWIC co-ordinate index: a new approach for preparation of high quality printed indexes by automatic indexing techniques* Ohio State University, Computer and Information Science Research Center 1969 (technical 69-7).

It should perhaps be noted that computer print-outs of key-word indexes *appear* to be more complex in make-up than the examples of such indexes given above. However, examination of both will reveal that the same principles have been adhered to.

Lastly, as previously indicated on p 150, it should again be pointed out that key-word from title indexes can be 'enriched' by the inclusion of additional indexing terms.

Post-coordinate indexing

Dr Mortimer Taube ' Uniterms in co-ordinate indexing' *American documentation* 3 (4) October 1952 213-218, and *Studies in co-ordinate indexing* volume one (Washington, Documentation Inc, 1953), developed the uniterm indexing system in the early fifties as a means of dealing with the mass of research reports, derived from scientific research projects, pouring into the us Armed Services Technical Information Agency (ASTIA) at that time.

This system usually makes no attempt to impose subject arrangement on the documents, each of which is given a simple serial (or accession) number, and filed in sequence. As originally proposed, the indexer freely extracts from the words in the title, abstract, or text, a list of those words which are considered indicative of the subject content. Relationship and sequence of one term to another is ignored, and all chosen terms are treated as having equal value and are established as separate headings or ' unit terms ' on the entries in the index. Each ' term ' card will carry, in a pattern made more orderly by the employment of numbered columns, a display of the numbers of all documents for which the index term has been chosen. Thus, for example, document 66 on the subject 'the teaching of mathematics in universities' will have separate entries for 'teaching', for 'mathematics' and for 'universities', each entry bearing the number 66—'posted' or entered in the column appropriate to the last digit in the number. The latter is known as 'terminal digital posting' and is a device to facilitate searches by comparison. Using the index then involves the searcher in selecting the descriptive terms for his subject, removing the appropriate term cards and scanning them for a common number.

TEACHING									
0	1	2	3	4	5	6	7	8	9
						66			

MATHEMATICS									
0	1	2	3	4	5	6	7	8	9
						66			

UNIVERSITIES									
0	1	2	3	4	5	6	7	8	9
						66			

The term cards are co-ordinates in the system and the location of sought documents is indicated at 'the intersection of the co-ordinates', being the number or numbers found common to all of them. In a 'manual' system the numbers are 'written' in but in an 'optical co-incidence' system the numbers are indicated by holes punched in certain positions. Cards can then be compared by holding them up to the light (hence 'peek-a-boo' cards) or by placing them on a light box. The light will 'shine through' if there is a common number on all the cards being compared.

Amongst the advantages claimed for the method are: 1 the speed of filing the document (no need to assign a complex classification notation); 2 faster indexing, with indexer using terms available in title and text; 3 faster searching since each term entry carries *all* relevant numbers on the one term card, unlike the more conventional catalogue ' item entry ' with one document description per card; 4 facility with which the system can be used by mechanical indexing methods (see also p 161, 162, 163, 167).

Criticisms include: 1 accession number order of documents means approach must *always* be made in the index, direct access to, or browsing in, the document collection not being possible (unless an 'accessions register' is compiled as an intermediary but this involves the disadvantage of an extra record); 2 the 'simplicity' of using ' title-available ' language is more apparent than real, *ie* ambiguity of terms, synonyms, generic to specific relationships, create real difficulties; 3 a high percentage of ' false drops ' can occur, for example a document on 'The history of teaching' could be retrieved in response to a request for information on the teaching of history. Such retrieval of irrelevant information is referred to as 'noise' and this may be reduced by 'role' indicators, *eg* History (as subject of study) *and* History (of a subject), or Orange (colour) *and* Orange (fruit). Another device to eliminate noise is the 'link', which connects related terms within the context of a document. A document on African elephants and Indian tigers should not be retrieved in response to a search for information on Indian elephants. Such retrieval can be avoided by numbering 'Africa' and 'elephants'—54 and 'India' and 'tigers'—54A, thus 'linking' the related terms.

Terminological difficulties have led later developments and modifications in co-ordinate indexing towards the production of dictionaries of ' controlled uniterms ', or ' thesauri of descriptors ' which simply represent a move towards establishing an accepted and agreed vocabulary for the indexer (and the searcher). This strongly reflects the conventional alphabetical subject catalogue's progression from subject ' catchword ' entry derived from title to the use of established lists of subject headings.

Well known examples of thesauri are the Engineers' Joint Council *Thesaurus of engineering and scientific terms,* the English

Electric *Thesaurofacet* and *MeSH* (*Medical Subject Headings*), published with each January issue of *Index medicus* and used as a basis of the MEDLARS system (see p 170).

Application of post-coordinate indexing in a wide variety of document collections, using an extensive array of manual and mechanical methods and equipment, has been reported in innumerable articles. An account, which includes discussion on the pros and cons of the system, is to be found in J C Costello *Co-ordinate indexing* (New Brunswick, Rutgers University Press 1966). L Jolley has discussed the method in ' The mechanics of co-ordinate indexing' ASLIB *Proceedings* 15 (6) June 1963 161-169. *Bakewell* (p 232-238) provides a short but very readable and informative account of the method.

COM (see p 32-34) has led to proposals being put forward for the computer production of a manually usable adjunct or index to an automated information retrieval system using optical coincidence principles. Microfiche, overprinted with a grid, can be employed as feature cards, with 'holes' represented by transparent areas on a black or dark-grey background of film. See 'COMP: Computer Output Microfilm Peek-a-boo ', by R A Wall *Library Association record* 74 (3) March 1972 44-45.

It is possible to print out post-coordinate indexes in book form, *provided* that at least two copies of the index are available. They can then be laid side by side and entries compared for common numbers. Such an index is known as a *dual dictionary*.

Pre-coordinate and post-coordinate indexing compared

The difference between the subject approach in pre-coordinate and post-coordinate indexes should perhaps be stressed now.

In post-coordinate indexing, the number of entries in the index is usually equal to the number of concepts or elements that together make up the full context of the subject. 'The *teaching* of *mathematics* in *universities*' required three entries only. The *co-ordination* was carried out at the search stage and citation order was irrelevant.

In a pre-coordinate index, the complete context of the subject must be shown and the various ways in which the concepts which make up the subject can be manipulated or permuted by the indexer decrees that numerous entries may be necessary. For the above example there are six possible permutations, *ie*

Teaching: Mathematics: Universities
Teaching: Universities: Mathematics
Mathematics: Teaching: Universities
Mathematics: Universities: Teaching
Universities: Teaching: Mathematics
Universities: Mathematics: Teaching

The number of entries required can be calculated by the formula $n \times (n-1) \times (n-2) \times (n-3)$ etc, where n = the number of concepts present. In the above instance, the calculation would be $3 \times (3-1) \times (3-2)$ *ie* $3 \times 2 \times 1 = 6$. It can be seen that the number of entries required rapidly increases as the subject becomes more complex. For a subject containing only seven concepts, full permutation to cover all possible approaches would lead to an incredible 5,040 entries. This is obviously completely unacceptable, whether an index is being compiled for a library catalogue or for some other information retrieval system.

It follows, therefore, that a post-coordinate system has the advantage of a smaller number of entries to give the same coverage. With pre-coordinate indexes, the problem has always been how to *reduce* the number of entries whilst retaining an acceptable degree of efficiency in the system.

Pre-coordinate indexing methods

Two ways in which a reduction in the number of entry points in a pre-coordinate index can be achieved have already been examined. These are 'chain' indexing and the 'shunting' procedure used in PRECIS. Other methods include:

Cycled or cyclic indexing which involves the movement of the first *lead* term to the last position and this process is continued until each element or concept has occupied the lead position once.

Rotated indexing. In this method each element in turn becomes the main heading under which an entry is to be filed but there is no change in the citation order. The main heading element is indicated by underlining.

SLIC indexing, or Selective Listing in Combination, involves the combination of elements in *one direction only* and the exclusion of combinations which are contained in larger groups.

The principles underlying these methods may be demonstrated

by taking as an example a subject containing three elements which are represented by A, B and C.

The entries obtained would be as follows:

Chain: **A B C**   PRECIS: A B C   Cycling: A B C
          B C   B C   B C A
          C   A   C A B
                          C
                          B A

Rotation: *A* B C   SLIC: A B C
            A *B* C   A C
            A B *C*   B C
                              C

Now taking an actual example, 'the cleaning of the upholstery of a chair', the various entries would be:

Chain: Cleaning: Upholstery: Chairs
                  Upholstery: Chairs
                  Chairs
PRECIS: **Cleaning.** Upholstery. Chairs
                  Upholstery. Chairs
                    Cleaning
                  Chairs
                  Upholstery. Cleaning
Cycling: Cleaning: Upholstery: Chairs
                  Upholstery: Chairs: Cleaning
                  Chairs: Cleaning: Upholstery
Rotation: Cleaning: Upholstery: Chairs
                  Cleaning: Upholstery: Chairs
                  Cleaning: Upholstery: Chairs
SLIC: Cleaning: Upholstery: Chairs
                  Cleaning: Chairs
                  Upholstery: Chairs
                  Chairs

The above examples are intended only as an *illustration* of the application of the various methods. In practice there would be other factors involved, for instance the 'chain' would be provided by the classification scheme in use. In addition, in a system such as PRECIS, references might also be required.

Several further points are worthy of note:

i In Chain, PRECIS and SLIC, element citation order plays an important role.

ii Indexes such as SLIC are intended mainly for use in computerised systems.

iii There is a close relationship between the rotated index and KWIC indexing (see p 150).

OTHER INDEXING TECHNIQUES

Automatic indexing

By removing the human intellectual element from indexing and allowing the computer to select terms suitable for indexing, a form of automatic indexing is obtained. But how does the computer identify appropriate terms? Originally this was done by determining, statistically, the words which occurred most frequently in a document (excluding common words) but later techniques have evolved around the selection of sentences. Sentences are weighted according to predetermined measures of significance. Sentences with the highest weights are likely to be those which best summarise the subject content of the document.

C D Batty considers 'The automatic generation of index languages' in *Journal of documentation* 25 (2) June 1969 142-151.

Key-words and clumps

At the Cambridge Language Research Unit, research has been carried out in an attempt to construct a classification of key-words based on the way in which terms 'co-occur' in documents. Terms thus related are grouped together into 'clumps'.

A number of articles by K Sparck Jones and others have dealt with this research. Beginning with *Journal of documentation* 20 (1) March 1964 5-15 and continuing with *Information storage and retrieval* 4 (2) June 1968 91-100 and 5 (4) February 1970 175-201; *Aslib proceedings* 22 (5) May 1970 226-228. These articles were followed up in 1971 with a book by Sparck Jones entitled *Automatic keyword classification for information retrieval* (London, Butterworth: Hamden, Conn, Archon 1971). *Foskett* (p 402-404) provides a brief review of the method.

Articulated subject indexing

Articulated subject indexing which was developed by Michael Lynch and his colleagues at the University of Sheffield Postgraduate School of Librarianship and Information Science, involves the manipulation, by a computer, of a natural language sentence describing the subject of a document to bring certain elements to the file position in turn. Unlike most other indexing methods, prepositions and conjunctions, etc are not discarded but used, sometimes as signals instructing the computer to print out in a certain manner. Brackets are also used for this purpose, so that the input:

[Standards] for [testing] of [fabrics]

would be manipulated by the computer to obtain the index entries:

> fabrics
> > testing of, standards for
> standards
> > for testing of fabrics
> testing
> > of fabrics, standards

The simple example given above illustrates that the system is designed to enable the searcher to reconstruct the sentence with the minimum of effort and this is still possible with far more complex sentences.

Michael Lynch describes the method in 'Computer-organised display of subject information' *Indexer* 7 (3) Spring 1971 94-100. The practical application of the method is considered in 'Computer aided production of the subject index to the SMRE bibliography', by M Belton (*Indexer* 8 (1) April 1972 44-49).

Citation indexing

If a person knows that a certain article is concerned with a particular subject field in which he is interested, then articles which *cite* that relevant article in a list of references are also likely to be of interest. This is the principle upon which citation indexing operates. Citations are sorted automatically by computer and alphabetical listings under authors *cited* and sources, that is *citing* authors, are compiled.

The best known index of this nature is *Science citation index*, which should be examined, and a useful article on the method is 'Citation indexing', by John Martyn *Indexer* 5 (1) Spring 1966 5-15.

When citation indexing is considered, note must be taken of *bibliographic coupling*. Two articles are *coupled* if they both cite the *same* additional article as a reference. Obviously the strength of the coupling increases according to the number of common references and when this is considerable then it is likely that the two articles deal with very much the same subject.

Search strategy

As persons requiring information often find it difficult to express themselves clearly, then obviously the first essential is that they be diplomatically encouraged and gently 'guided' in order that as complete and clear a statement as possible is obtained. As *Foskett* (p 198) states, 'the *reference interview* is an important part of any information retrieval process'.

After the 'interview', the enquiry must be translated into suitable descriptive terms which can be put to the information system and relevant material identified. If there are 'hard' identifying factors such as document authors or titles then little difficulty will be encountered. The system should provide a straight 'yes' or 'no' answer. Subject searches, however, are not quite so simple.

A subject which can be represented by a single concept, *eg* 'mathematics' will be relatively easy to handle, but complex subjects are more problematic. When searching in a pre-coordinate index, the user looks first for the heading or index entry representing the complete context of the subject required, *eg* Teaching : Mathematics : Universities. The subject can be presented in a number of ways, as previously indicated, Mathematics : Teaching : Universities; Universities : Teaching : Mathematics, and so on. It is obviously not sufficient to consult only one of these as many indexing techniques do not preserve the complete subject context at all entry points. An examination of the documents listed or the information given under a particular heading, or at a particular location indicated by the index, may or may not provide the answer to the enquiry. If nothing suitable is found at the heading chosen, the user will consult other headings, perhaps synonymous with, related to, or progressively more general than the first choice, making use of any appropriate references or other guiding. Proceeding in this way, information relevant to the enquiry may eventually be traced, although the *degree* of relevance will vary according to the material available and whether such material is present in the system.

In post-coordinate systems, elements present in a complex subject must be searched for individually. Concept cards are extracted and compared in order to identify common numbers which *may* relate to documents relevant to the enquiry. Searches can be 'broadened' by reducing the number of concepts or elements. If a search is begun using four concepts, for example, each of the four could be disregarded in turn. Thus a search could be conducted using various combinations of only three of the concepts.

No one search strategy will serve for all information systems, it will vary from system to system or even from search to search according to the type of system or the requirement of the user. It can be seen, however, that the process of subject searching involves a manipulation of concepts. The context of a subject can be enlarged or reduced according to the manner in which concepts are combined or related. Taking the concepts 'teaching' and 'mathematics' as an example, what could be called the 'product' of these concepts could be searched for producing all documents dealing with the 'teaching of mathematics'. This could be represented pictorially by using two circles, circle 'A' for all documents on 'teaching' and circle 'B' for all those on 'mathematics'. The shaded area indicates the search requirement.

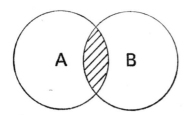

Logical *product*—the 'and' search
Symbolised as A.B, A x B or (A) (B)
All documents dealing with 'mathematics' and 'teaching'

It may well be that what is required is all documents dealing with 'teaching' and/or 'mathematics', that is on 'mathematics' only, on 'teaching' only, or with both 'teaching and mathematics'. This situation could again be represented pictorially.

Lastly a search could be made for all documents dealing with 'mathematics' excluding those covering the 'teaching of mathematics'.

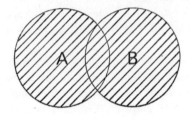

Logical *sum*—the 'or' search
Symbolised as $A + B$
All documents on 'teaching'
or 'mathematics'

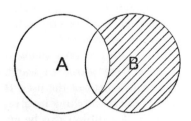

Logical *difference*—the 'not' search
Symbolised as $A - B$
All documents on 'mathematics' but *not* 'the teaching of mathematics'

The value of the latter search is limited, as it can result in failure to retrieve relevant documents. For example, if a search is being conducted on the pattern;

'Computers' and 'Information retrieval systems' not 'Chemistry' the document ' Computerised information retrieval systems in physics and chemistry', which is relevant, would be rejected.

Conversely, in post-coordinate systems, the logical product is obviously of prime importance.

The above 'Venn' diagrams are pictorial representations based on the Boolean algebra of sets. They have been found to be extremely useful as illustrations of coordination in information retrieval. Using 'search logic' in this way, search 'patterns' can be developed. A typical pattern might be:

$$\left(\begin{array}{c} A \\ or \\ B \end{array} \right) \quad and \quad \left(\begin{array}{c} A_1 \\ or \\ B_1 \end{array} \right) \quad not \quad \left(\begin{array}{c} A_2 \\ or \\ B_2 \end{array} \right)$$

For instance, if information were required on the classification and cataloguing of maps and charts, excluding atlases or globes, then the search pattern could be displayed graphically as:

$$\left(\begin{array}{c} Cataloguing \\ or \\ Classification \end{array} \right) \quad and \quad \left(\begin{array}{c} Maps \\ or \\ Charts \end{array} \right) \quad not \quad \left(\begin{array}{c} Atlases \\ or \\ Globes \end{array} \right)$$

In automated systems, where the human intellectual element is not present and the computer merely does as it is instructed, the value of such search formulations becomes obvious.

With regard to automated systems, another useful device is 'truncation'. If a search is made on 'cataloguing', then items indexed under 'catalogues' will be 'missed'. Searching on the truncation 'catalog', however, will ensure that material indexed in both ways is retrieved. It will be seen that this is most useful in natural language systems. Searching for the truncation or word stem 'classif' obviates the necessity for the formulation of a search pattern such as 'classification' or classificatory' or 'classifier' or 'classified'.

Search strategy is dealt with in various sections of *Foskett*. A more advanced treatment of the subject will be found in Gilchrist (*op cit* ch 9); Lancaster (*op cit* p 70-74 and ch 15), and Vickery *Techniques . . . (op cit* ch 12).

Testing and evaluation of information retrieval systems

When considering the testing and evaluation of information systems, certain terms now in common use must first be defined.These terms are 'specificity', 'exhaustivity', 'recall' and 'precision'.

Specificity The degree to which an information system allows the exact subject of a document to be specified.
Example: An information system caters only for the indexing of the general concept 'university education' without subdivision. It is impossible, therefore, to specify a subject such as 'the use of audio visual aids in the teaching of mathematics in universities'. The system lacks *specificity*.

Exhaustivity The extent to which the subject content of a document is analysed by the indexer.
Example: A document dealing with different breeds of dogs could simply be indexed under 'dogs' but the indexing could be made more *exhaustive* if each individual breed 'alsatians', 'boxers', 'dalmatians', etc was also indexed. This is known as *depth indexing*.

Recall The amount of material or number of documents produced in answer to an enquiry which meet, that is are relevant to, the requirements of the user.* The *recall ratio* is the ratio between the total number of documents present in the collection which are relevant to an enquiry and the number of these actually retrieved in a search.

Example: There are twenty documents relevant to an enquiry in an information system and fifteen are retrieved by a search. The recall ratio is therefore 75%.

Precision A measure of the relative efficiency of a system by a comparison of the number of *relevant* documents retrieved with the total number of documents, relevant or irrelevant, produced by the search.

Example: Referring to the example for recall, if there were, in fact, a further ten documents retrieved which were not relevant to the enquiry then the *precision ratio* would be $\dfrac{15}{15+10}=60\%$.

The terms are inter-related in that 'specificity' increases 'relevance' at the cost of 'recall' but 'exhaustivity' increases 'recall' and decreases 'relevance' (although each index term could be 'weighted', that is allocated a number which would indicate degree of relevance). It could be claimed, perhaps with some justification, that the introduction of these terms is simply a case of a new tune played on an old fiddle. It has long been apparent that 'specificity increases relevance but reduces recall' as the following example illustrates. If an enquirer asks for information on budgerigars and a search is made under that specific term, few documents will be produced but they will all be highly relevant. A search under the broader term 'cage birds' would obviously produce more items but these would not be so relevant and a search under the even wider term 'pets' would produce a great number of items but many of these would obviously not be relevant at all.

Lancaster (*op cit*) provides detailed information on the testing and evaluation of information retrieval systems. *Foskett* (ch 23 'Research in information retrieval') is also useful.

---

* It could be considered that *recall* relates to the *total number* of documents retrieved, *whether relevant or irrelevant*. However, as explained here, recall relates only to those retrieved documents which are *relevant*. This would appear to agree with the general consensus of opinion amongst the major textbooks and also with the draft British Standard *Glossary of documentation terms*. In this glossary, recall is defined as the 'retrieval of a *required* document or its reference from an information store'. (The italics are mine.)

The Cranfield project

An important comparative testing of some of the systems of subject cataloguing and information retrieval was carried out at the College of Aeronautics at Cranfield, in Bedfordshire, UK. The project was directed by C W Cleverdon for ASLIB and financed by the National Science Foundation. The four systems tested were: 1 alphabetical subject catalogue, using a subject headings list: 2 UDC classified catalogue with an alphabetical index to UDC numbers; 3 classified catalogue arranged by a specially constructed faceted scheme with a chain index; 4 a uniterm co-ordinate index using an ' authority ' list of uniterms. As well as the system, such variables as the indexer, the indexer's rate of learning and the indexing time were tested. The work of indexing 18,000 documents (half in the field of high-speed aerodynamics, half in the general field of aeronautics) by the four systems took three indexers two years. Some 1,200 ' test questions ' were put to each of the four systems and the results statistically analysed.

C W Cleverdon's *Report on the first stage of an investigation into the comparative efficiency of indexing systems* (College of Aerodynamics, Cranfield 1960) and *Report on the testing and analysis of an investigation* (1962) provide the basis for the excellent account given by B C Vickery *On retrieval system theory* (London, Butterworths second edition 1965) p 168-177. Vickery tabulates the conclusions concisely on p 170-171. Some of the findings indicate that: 1 the recall ratio percentage of sought documents successfully retrieved) of all four systems was very close (although the chain index on the faceted system had to be modified to bring it up to a level comparable with the others); 2 ' there was no significant difference in the case of retrieving items indexed by different indexers '; 3 increased time spent on indexing improved the chance of recall; 4 faulty indexing caused sixty per cent of the failures to retrieve source documents (the others being caused by question failures (seventeen per cent), searching failures (seventeen per cent), system failures (six per cent)).

In the light of the project's failure to provide a clear answer to the basic question of which system *was* the most effective, a second ASLIB-Cranfield project was mounted, confining itself to studying *the methods* which might be employed to test the efficiency of various retrieval systems. The first report of Cranfield II is contained in C W Cleverdon *and others Factors determining the performance of indexing systems, Vol 1: Design* (Cranfield, 1966).

The Aberystwyth project

A further investigation into indexing systems was carried out at the College of Librarianship Wales, beginning in 1968. Various types of indexing languages, including post-coordinate and faceted schemes, were tested using a collection of items in the fields of library science and documentation. The results have now been published: E M Keen and J A Digger *Report of information science index languages test* (Aberystwyth, College of Librarianship 2v 1972). This detailed and comprehensive report states that the conclusion reached was as follows:

'The languages tested did not often exhibit significant differences in retrieval performance effectiveness and efficiency, and no really large differences were observed'.

A further conclusion, based upon the controlled versus the uncontrolled language controversy was that:

'The uncontrolled languages tested performed overall just as well as the controlled languages by providing a consistently good retrieval effectiveness and efficiency performance that was never as bad as the worst controlled language, nor as good as the best, and in no case were these differences statistically significant'.

More detailed findings concerned with specificity, exhaustivity and precision are also included in the report but the basic conclusion is similar to that of the Cranfield project in that no one system was found to be significantly better than any other.

Manual, mechanical, electronic equipment

The modern cataloguer or indexer may make use of a considerable range of equipment, varying from the simple typewriter to the much more complex computer. Examples of the use of equipment such as tape typewriters, addressing machines, cameras, copiers and the computer itself have already been cited. A further example is 'telex', which involves the transmission and automatic reception of typed messages via the normal telephone system. To cite one example of its application to cataloguing methods, telex can afford speedy access to central records, thus obviating the necessity for branch library catalogues, as in Buckinghamshire (see

Foskett is extremely useful for all aspects of the subject approach to information.

Other more specialised works include:

Gilchrist, Alan: *The thesaurus in retrieval* (London, Aslib 1971).

Lancaster, F W: *Information retrieval systems: characteristics, testing and evaluation* (London, Wiley 1968).

Sharp, J R: *Some fundamentals of information retrieval* (London, Deutsch 1965). 'The shortcomings of conventional systems' (ch 4) are contrasted with 'The advantages of non-conventional systems' (ch 5).

Vickery, B C: *Techniques of information retrieval* (London, Butterworth 1970). A more advanced work by the same author is *On retrieval theory* (London, Butterworth: Hamden, Conn, Archon 2nd ed 1965).

Michael J Ramsden has written *An introduction to index language construction* (London, Bingley 1974), which is a programmed guide to compiling a structured index language.

A review of mechanical aids used in library work is given in ch 13 of:

Ashworth, W ed: *Handbook of special librarianship and information work* (London, Aslib 3rd ed 1967).

CHAPTER ELEVEN

PAST ACHIEVEMENTS AND FUTURE PROSPECTS

In recent years astonishing progress has been made in the information retrieval field. Some of the systems, methods and technical developments mentioned in this book are outstanding achievements which have made and are making significant contributions. The Ohio College Library Center system, BLCMP, Laser, Brimarc, Books in English, PRECIS and COM are examples which immediately spring to mind.

MEDLARS

Behind many of these achievements lies the computer, and it has been, perhaps, the MEDLARS system (MEDical Literature Analysis and Retrieval System) cf the US National Library of Medicine which has exhibited so far the most dramatic demonstration of computer capabilities in both bibliographical control and indexing. The system is designed to provide access to articles in over 2,300 biomedical journals from 1964 to date. The data base for MEDLARS is the same as that used to create *Index medicus* and *International nursing index* and is world wide in scope.

In response to a request for a MEDLARS search, the enquirer will receive, after an interval of two-three weeks, a list of references printed out by the computer. The user can then obtain copies of the articles he requires through the usual library channels. MEDLARS is suitable for the solving of complex problems, when it is necessary to search for references under several subject headings, and also for problems which involve aspects of articles not retrievable by the subject headings in the printed indexes, for example common laboratory or clinical techniques. Experiments are being carried out at present with regard to on-line access to the MEDLARS store.

A J Harley has compiled a handbook for the users of the UK

MEDLARS: *UK MEDLARS information service* . . . (Boston Spa, National Lending Library 2nd ed 1968). A useful article is 'MEDLARS: a summary review and evaluation of three reports', by Norman D Stevens *Library resources and technical services* 14 (1) Winter 1970 109-121.

There are of course many other computer-based information services. Examples are the American Chemical Society's Chemical Abstracts Service (CAS) and, in the UK, the Information Service in Physics, Electrotechnology and Control (INSPEC), operated by the Institution of Electrical Engineers. A useful list of computer-based systems is *A guide to selected computer-based information services*, compiled by Ruth Finer (London, Aslib 1972).

Library of Congress

Apart from MEDLARS, the 'other great event in recent library history', as Coblans has referred to it, has been the progress that the Library of Congress has made towards automation, bringing with it the development of project MARC, which has already been discussed in some detail.

LC automation activities are based on the report by G W King *and others Automation and the Library of Congress* (Washington, LC 1963) which is concisely summarised by B E Markuson 'The United States Library of Congress automation survey' UNESCO *Bulletin for libraries* 19 (11) Jan-Feb 1965 24-34.

The picture has been up-dated in various articles written since that time and current activity is described in reports on developments at the Library of Congress which appear in its *Information bulletin.*

As part of the plans for the systematic automation of technical processes in LC, considerable progress has been made on the Multiple Use MARC System (MUMS), which will be capable of using either disc or tapes for peripheral storage and will have on-line and off-line capabilities. The first application scheduled to operate under MUMS in 1974 is the redesign of the MARC input system. The first phase will allow on-line corrections to MARC records. Further more ambitious phases are planned, including an Automated Process Information File (APIF). APIF will eventually provide for on-line searching and ultimately the project will be expanded to cover languages other than English and material other than books.

LC's role as a principal centre for the transmission of machine-readable data, taken in conjunction with its emergence as a global centre for the collection and transmission of catalogue data from similar centres in other countries through the Shared Cataloguing Programme, promises to open up an entirely new era for bibliographical control and cataloguing.

The future

The processes of automation offer endless possibilities for the improvement and integration of library operations and, inevitably, this book will quickly date as further developments take place.

There seems no doubt that the number of cataloguers required at a local level will be reduced dramatically as centralised services become more efficient and more economic. Whether existing staffs will be redeployed on other tasks (see also p 140) remains to be seen but it seems obvious that the library schools will need to reconsider the emphasis that is now placed on the teaching of practical cataloguing and indexing. The subject must not, however, be allowed to disappear altogether from our professional syllabuses. A librarian, even if not engaged in practical work, must understand and be able to examine critically the systems that he uses or intends to use.

Where other future developments are concerned, there is even speculation that the physical form of books and other materials could be abandoned and their contents transferred to the vast memory of the computer, the 'bits' being efficiently labelled for identification, indexed, and stored (*ie* catalogued), to be recalled, considered, compared, used, enriched, and re-filed by multiple users, each at his own console. Such is the kind of picture which has emerged from various works over the past decade. An early experiment of this nature, which is still continuing and which envisages an unlimited number of users linked nation-wide to a large central computer, is Project INTREX (INformation TRansfer EXperiment). The possible prospects for such a system are considered by J C R Licklider in *Libraries of the future* (Cambridge (Mass), MIT Press 1965).

On the other hand, presuming that the book and document as a physical form will persist for a long time ahead (and this is not an unreasonable assumption if only in respect of the sheer numbers of these items), there is yet the possibility that libraries will be seen as a network of document-centred communications storage systems, linked and operated by sophisticated computer methods which may make today's catalogues seem quite primitive instruments.

Whatever the future may bring, there can be little doubt but that any developments will owe much to the theory and practice of cataloguing, evolved by librarians for the systematic organisation of books, documents, and bibliographical records.

READINGS

Bakewell Ch 16 'The future of cataloguing'.

Foskett Part V 'Future prospects'.

SUBJECT INDEX

INDEX OF AUTHORS CITED

The terms or phrases in parentheses indicate the context in which the article or reading has been cited in the text, and do not represent exact title or subject. The full bibliographical details are given on the page indicated.

Catalogues — other aspects
then says. Centralised services.
= less. Not even convinced
that it can be.